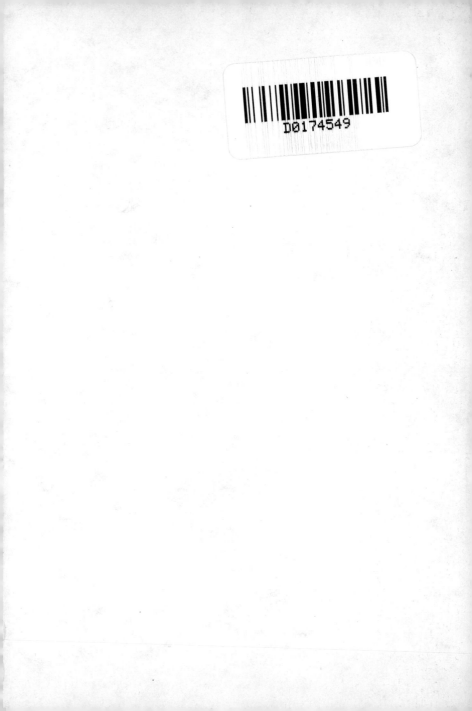

RICH
with
YEARS

DAILY MEDITATIONS
ON GROWING OLDER

Malcolm Boyd

HarperSanFrancisco
A Division of HarperCollins*Publishers*

FIRST EDITION

Library of Congress Cataloging-in-Publication Data
Boyd, Malcolm.
Rich with years : daily meditations on growing older / Malcolm Boyd.
p.   cm.
Includes index.
ISBN 0–06–250258–1 (alk. paper)
1. Aged—Prayer-books and devotions—English.
2. Devotional calendars.
I. Title
BL625.4.B68   1994   93–11337
291.4'3—dc20   CIP

94 95 96 97 ❖ BANVA 10 9 8 7 6 5 4 3 2 1

This edition is printed on acid-free paper that meets the American National Standards Institute Z39.48 Standard.

To my mother, Beatrice Boyd,
in her triumphant ninety-fifth year

I express grateful acknowledgment to all the men and women, including readers of my "You and I" column in *Modern Maturity* magazine, who have kindly written me remarkably honest letters in which they have shared their thoughts and feelings. I particularly want to thank Kevin Bentley for his skillful editing of this book.

Beauty, strength, youth, are flowers but fading seen;
Duty, faith, love, are roots, and ever green.

GEORGE PEELE, "HIS GOLDEN LOCKS TIME HATH
TO SILVER TURNED"

RICH
with
YEARS

Getting older is an adventure, not a problem.

BETTY FRIEDAN

What a splendid adventure it really is. It beckons us, and will require all our energy and vision, hope and grit, patience and love.

Most of us have been told, however, that getting older is a problem, not an adventure. We were offered harrowing images of hopeless, decrepit men and women. Youth was held up as the perfect role model; age was depicted as forlorn, embarrassing, and ugly. The wisdom of age was greeted with contempt: What wisdom?

As human liberation movements begin to grow and flourish, getting older may finally come to be seen in a new light of adventure, growth, and expectation. Growing older is not an option. It is a given. Yet how we grow older is a definite option. Doing it well requires a mix of hard pragmatism and gentle serenity, wise self-assertion and a trust in community, a firm pride in being an elder leavened with the humility of one who genuinely wishes to share old truths with an emerging new generation.

Today, I will try looking at my life as an adventure. I am ready for a challenge.

They're having an age problem. He won't act his, she won't tell hers.

MILTON BERLE

Our age is perfectly obvious to most people, unless we happen to be an aging movie star with a face lift.

This is true whether or not we announce or act our age. Deliberately setting out to camouflage our age is a precarious game. Disaster threatens at every turn. What if a wig flies off in the wind? Makeup runs in the rain? A corset pops? Or, as in the film *Lost Horizon,* old people who looked very young suddenly show their age?

It's a smart idea to wear our age with good taste and dignity, in health and style, wherever possible. On the one hand, if we are proud of our age and content to be ourself, why hide it? On the other hand, if we're ashamed of our age and unwilling to be ourself, this reflects deep problems that need to be unraveled. Let's tell our age, act it, laugh with it, and enjoy it.

Today, I'll wear my years like a fine linen suit. And I'll act exactly how I feel.

JANUARY 2

I've always had friends much younger than myself. I'm in my seventies now, and I have a group of friends in their twenties and thirties who seem to like my stories, who take me out and spoil me. Sometimes, though, I wonder if they just want to inherit my house.

Friendships across lines of ethnicity, race, sex, and age are the most natural things in the world. They should be enjoyed and celebrated. They reaffirm what is best about the human spirit.

However, many of our lives have been touched by prejudice of one sort or another, including negative attitudes toward people who are different from us. Often we've been taught to fear them. Or not to trust them. This is terribly unfortunate.

It's good to remember that the only thing we need fear is fear itself. This allows us to know other people as potential friends, not enemies; to be trusting; and to let go of debilitating thoughts that are harbingers of fear.

I'll take people as they are. I'll err on the side of trust. I can't waste the gift of a single friendship.

I had a real crisis at sixty. All my life I'd been active—worked, raised a family. Suddenly everything came to a dead halt. I ran out of energy and hope, and hated my life. Now, thank God, I am back on track. I'm taking an aerobics class, studying Spanish, and feel alive and happy to greet the new day. It's marvelous.

Life goes on and gets better when it is treated with affection, good sense, and obdurate determination.

Our opportunities for living richly and more fully are legion. Studying a foreign language, for example, is immensely helpful not only when visiting the land of its origin, but also for training the mind to remember. A class that involves the body physically—aerobics, dance, exercise, yoga—tunes up one's whole being.

These are the sort of things we should pursue at all ages and stages of our lives. It's as important in our thirties and forties as in our seventies. Sometimes we need a push or shove to get started in a new program for our mind and body. A challenge from a friend can be helpful. So can a firm resolution, and following through.

Life goes on. Today, I resolve to go with it.

Please don't retouch my wrinkles. It took me so long to earn them.

ANNA MAGNANI

We need to learn how to be proud of our signs of growing older. It's not always easy when those signs are ridiculed or criticized by the culture.

Wrinkles may be a part of life now, along with peppered or gray hair. We may move more slowly or run out of breath while trying to sustain a quick pace. An older man or woman may indeed stand out strikingly in a crowd.

Why is this so? Only because of these things?

No! There are other factors. An older person can possess a sense of dignity that often comes with age, and a poise not unlike that of an old oak tree that has weathered many seasons. There may be an attitude of ease and innate relaxation indicating that such a person has reached an understanding about life, a victory over vicissitudes, a peace that is ennobling.

Today, I'll face the world with pride. I've earned it.

Retirement is simply another form of challenge, but a delightful one because for once I get to make the rules. I get to decide just how fulfilling or empty my life will be.

Isn't it wonderful to be able to make a choice? Imagine we're in a forest, night is falling, and our path suddenly breaks into two different directions. Which one to take? The decision is terribly important and could be a life-or-death choice.

So is our choice about whether our life will be empty or fulfilling. This is our choice. An empty life is a selfish one. It exists when we shut out the rest of the world, creating a tiny semblance of a universe that caters exclusively to what we assume are our needs. A fulfilling life, on the other hand, is a shared one. We relate to different people, offer help, listen, and practice what's called empathy. The rules are finally up to us. There is no longer any authority figure telling us what to do, or even offering suggestions.

Retirement is an enormous challenge—and opportunity. We may become active in ways we never imagined, and also allow time for creative solitude. Why not occasionally sit under a friendly tree and meditate like the saints?

Today, I'll think about my choices. And then I'll choose.

There comes a time when you realize there are only fifty-two weekends a year, and the years are rushing by.

WILLIAM ATTWOOD

Exactly. Act 1 is past. Act 2 is moving right along. Sometime ahead the curtain will fall, the crowd will file out, the theater will be dark. What are we to do with our awareness that the years are rushing by?

Remember, there's a scene still in progress. We still have lines to speak, actions to perform. Indeed, the dénouement of the plot has not yet been revealed. So there's an enormous amount of work that remains to be done by us. Meanwhile, the audience continues to demand more, we're up on the stage with a responsibility to go on, and needless to say, our relationship with the other performers (quite aside from the people in the audience) has simply not yet been resolved.

Do you get the picture? We are unable to step outside the scene. It is still in motion. We're engrossed in the action and, if the truth be known, continue to find it terribly exciting. Our challenge is to see it through to completion, in top form.

Today, I'll give Act 2 my all. I'll script The End when it comes.

To fill a void in my life I decided to pursue an old dream. I looked for something I'd always loved and wanted to do, but never attempted.

We needn't always concentrate on having a new dream. An old dream may be especially informative, once we've dreamed it for a long time.

There are special things all of us have wanted to do, but the moment for them never came. These may range from learning a foreign language to writing poems, from playing a cello to doing volunteer work with disenfranchised kids, from becoming a priest to taking up archery, from dancing to joining a cooking school, from completing a long-abandoned degree to taking up painting.

A big question is: What did we never attempt that interested us? It might be climbing Mt. Everest but could also include performance art at a nearby community college, writing one's life story for children in the family, planting an herb garden, or rising very, very early to watch birds.

Today, I'll dream an old dream. Then I'll make it real.

Destiny always seems decades away, but suddenly it's not decades away; it's right now.

WALTER M. MILLER, JR

We remember turning twenty. It was a sign of growing up. We felt good about it.

However, thirty seemed to be another matter entirely. There was a different way to measure thirty. Had we made our first million? Built our dream house? Established a strong bridgehead for the rest of our life?

Forty was even harder. Forty! Many years ago a bestseller appeared under the title *Life Begins at Forty.* It created a sensation because everybody at that time assumed turning forty meant giving up. It didn't. Life still beckoned richly.

Fifty, sixty, seventy, eighty, and ninety are ages that hold vastly diverse meanings for different people. The truth seems to be: Life is where you find it. As the years turn like leaves, destiny is not a distant reality. It has a quality of immediacy. Decisions can no longer be shunted aside for a future reckoning. Happiness and contentment are of little value if they are only to be found over the rainbow. Human fulfillment is merely a mirage unless one actually reaches it.

Today, I'll stop waiting for life. My destiny is now.

I look awful, feel exhausted all the time, and am so lonely I could go bonkers. I can't turn my life around or go anywhere. Unless the heavens open up with miracles pouring down like rain, it looks hopeless for me.

A number of us feel this way on occasion. We lose perspective momentarily. We forget how really great we are. So we stop taking good care of ourselves, give in to misery, and accept a jury's negative verdict.

Yet there is neither a jury nor a verdict. Instead, there is only our own lack of confidence, absence of hope, and denial of the reality of goodness. Feeling sunk at certain moments is a universal experience. However, we're not sunk unless we believe we are.

Certainly, we cannot totally change our lives as if by magic. Yet we can make daily, significant changes. We can start healing depression, get rest or a new spark if we're tired out, reach out to others if we're lonely, fix up the way we look, get something to wear—and find a mirror, look into it, and smile. The message is: We can change *can't* to *want*.

What sort of miracle would it take to make me happy? Today, I'll picture that miracle. Then, I'll begin moving toward it.

JANUARY 10

Fatigue makes cowards of us all.

VINCE LOMBARDI

When we are fatigued we simply don't venture forth in the best of spirits, make the finest effort, or feel like taking significant risks. We don't feel like living fully.

The solution is: Combat fatigue in creative ways and try not to become its victim. If we need to take a rest, we should do precisely that. Or go for a restorative walk, work quietly in a garden, take an invigorating swim, maybe even get into a deep sleep for a few hours. It's important not to be too vain or obstinate to admit such a need. We must take care of the body as a prerequisite for taking care of the mind and the soul.

By reducing stress and working sensibly with fatigue, we can transform ourselves from a fearful and retiring creature to a self-reliant older person who accepts the disciplines of age with sturdy sense.

Today, I'll look for renewal. I will not let fatigue make me a coward.

When you're older, people expect you to be either a prude or a dirty old man. In fact, I'm as interested in sex as I ever was—and as disinterested.

When sex is identified solely with the rites of youth, it is ludicrously misunderstood.

Sex is as natural as breathing. It is a universal gift and an integral part of creation. But older women and men are frequently seen in an unnatural way and denied their humanity.

The stereotyping that takes place is both ridiculous and utterly wrong. "Older people are no longer sexual," it's affirmed. Or, "It's disgusting to see an older person who still spends time and energy on sex. Their minds should be on higher things unless they're dirty and perverted." Or the opposite: "Older people are judgmental, puritanical, rigid, and opposed to sex. They've forgotten what it means to be human." Our society stands in need of considerably more sex education and enlightenment. We need a lot more honesty and awareness.

I've a right to my loving thoughts. With love and encouragement, I'll express them

When my father was an old man, he surprised me by remarking that he understood what my mother's death meant to me but had no idea what to do about it.

WILLIAM MAXWELL

When life's secrets leap out at us unexpectedly, we're confronted with fresh understandings of past events.

Maybe everybody else at a big family gathering years ago knew the same secret about our grandmother, but we didn't—until now. Hearing it for the first time shocks us, opens old wounds, answers nagging questions. Why didn't we know? On deathbeds, many people are likely to speak their minds, tell secrets, place things at rest. When they do, the rest of us sometimes learn long-buried truths.

It can help everybody if we're able to share such things now instead of waiting. We might never have another chance. Revealed secrets have a healthful way of clarifying old paradoxes, answering questions, and contributing to better understanding. When they're shared, they contribute to loving, even if we're momentarily hurt in the process. It's better to know.

Today, I'll think twice about the secrets I keep. I will voice my love.

It's not important to me whether I'm worth one hundred million or twenty million or one hundred and fifty million. What I do need is a full life and doing the things that need to be done.

HUGH HEFNER

How do we measure the significance of our lives? It is a question all of us need to ask.

What is a full life? Definitions will vary according to a person's individual needs and desires. Some of us will place family and relationships first. Others will start with work fulfillment and recognition. Money may define the aspirations of others, along with creativity, sexual fulfillment, enjoyment of music and art, cooking and eating, and service to others.

Our own definition will largely determine the things we need to do in order to achieve what we call a full life. To be a caring, nurturing, loving person? To be a strong competitor? To be famous? To create art? To place ourself first? To place other people first? To be a great cook? To lead a life of personal satisfaction? To work long hours and become a business success? To lead a life of service to others? To smell flowers, hug trees, watch birds? The choice is our own.

Today, I'll think about what really *fulfills* my life. I'll head in that direction.

I'm old and physically helpless. I can't tie my shoes or feed myself. But I can visit a nursing home and talk to a friend who is in worse shape than I am.

In a world that sadly needs far more of them, we need all the stories we can find about human generosity and kindness.

When we reach out and help someone else, we're not only helping them. We're helping ourselves, too. We are becoming better persons. Our vistas grow wider instead of narrower. Self-interest makes room for interest beyond the self. Kindness is taking concrete form somewhere in the universe at this moment. Generosity becomes more than just a slogan, it is being practiced right now.

Some people ask, "Where can I find someone else who is in serious need of help?" Walk a city block among the homeless. Listen to people who are hungry. See loneliness a few seats away. Be aware of what people are not saying in their well-chosen, careful, often frightened words. These are the words of loved ones, friends, acquaintances, and strangers. Needs are all about us. We can commence by responding to one. Then, another. And another.

I'll leave off my own worries for a day. I'll try my hand at affecting another's life.

Forever getting-ready-for life instead of living it each day.

PETER MATTHIESSEN

Having reached a certain age, it becomes preposterous to postpone living any longer. If we don't get started, there won't be any time left. Why do we often resist living fully? Maybe we're lazy. Or else we're scared.

A deadline can help us. It prods us. It helps by making us feel guilty. One benefit of a deadline is that it thrusts us into the raw stuff of living, whether we feel like it or not. From a deadline at work to facing an important health decision, from cleaning the house to honoring a friendship, a deadline punctuates real life. Without a deadline of some kind, life can become a never-ending game or an irrelevant exercise in futility.

Actual living requires beginnings and endings, starts and finishes, getting ready and doing it.

I'll set myself a goal—and carry it out.

Silence, more than likely, is a stranger to your world, too.

WAYNE E. OATES

It's sad there is not more silence in the lives of most of us. We live amid a cacophony of sound, an explosion of noise pollution.

Yet even when we are surrounded by a volcanic eruption of discordant sounds, we can find silence within. Look inward. Turn inward. Find and nurture that secret garden where no one else goes. Spend some tender and lovely moments there. Get renewed energy. Then be prepared to go back into a world that demands our energy and resources.

It is not selfish to heal ourselves. If we neglect this vital work, we may hurt rather than help other people. Often we project our own sickness onto others, despite our good intentions to offer assistance. Our nerves may be frayed, emotions raw, bodies sick, souls in disarray. We should set aside quiet time for self-examination and healing.

I'll look for a still place. I'll sit and listen.

JANUARY 17

For forty-five years I blamed my lack of friends on the fact that I am overweight. Then I decided to be friendly toward people rather than wait for them. It worked. I found most people don't care about looks.

It can take a lifetime to make such a simple discovery. A big reason is that we live in a society where image is often considered more important than reality.

This, combined with the emergence of a youth cult in the media, leads to an emphasis on an unrealistic ideal of physical attractiveness. So being merely pretty takes precedence over being truly beautiful. Form is given credence over content. Many try to emulate or even become an image. This leads to tragedy when the self gets lost, despised, or rejected and a person becomes alienated from who he or she is.

The result is that we see a lot of robots running around, along with armies of stereotypes and legions of shadows on our streets. It's such a marvelous release to recognize that we are stunningly human, incredibly individual, fashioned in love, and free to be ourselves.

I'll look in the mirror and smile. I'll greet myself as I would someone I love

I am exhausted if I don't work.

PABLO PICASSO

It seems unlikely that the great artist Picasso was often bored. Even in his old age he usually had a dozen different projects on the fire.

What about us? Some of us are workaholics, never content to rest or play. But most of us have more leisure time as we grow older. The insistent demands of a stressful work life tend to be muted in retirement.

Does boredom become a new factor in daily living to be coped with? Don't be bored. Volunteer some of your energy and time to a needy cause. Find a task that is a good fit for your skills. Take a class and learn something new, especially in a subject that either interested or eluded you in the past. Play a musical instrument, collect stamps, cook good meals, visit a gym regularly, walk, swim, make a library your second home, go to a discussion group, sign up to work in an election. Stay active.

I will work against boredom.

JANUARY 19

I find that the habit of despair is a bottomless pit. I wonder if I can achieve the habit of hope instead?

Hope is always possible—but a change in focus is necessary. If we stare into a bottomless pit of despair, we cannot at the same time be looking with anticipation into the bright face of hope.

Sometimes we need to look away from the bottomless pit of despair. This requires an act of will or at least our being open to distraction. Even a firecracker exploding can provide a moment's release from the absorption of the stare into a bottomless pit. A moment's release is all that is required.

A change of focus is one of the great gifts of life. In a moment's flash, we can gain a new view, a fresh perspective, an actual change. Something, or everything, suddenly looks different: just like that! Where there was absolute hopelessness, now there is absolute possibility. We have all experienced this, but not often enough. We should make it a habit to change focus.

Today, I'll look at my life in a new way. Where there is hope, I will find it.

There comes a time when one must take the position that it is neither safe nor politic nor popular, but one must do it because human conscience says it is right.

MARTIN LUTHER KING, JR

We need to stand for something basically good in our lives. Our lives cry out for intrinsic meaning.

It is not enough to live cut off from the desperate problems and burdens of other people. Human life is a vast network comprising a universe of diverse people in myriad and perplexing situations. Wisely, John Donne reminded us in his classic lines that we should not ask for whom the bell tolls. It tolls for us, for each of us.

We can help one another in this life rather than remaining aloof and disinterested. Offer hope and tangible assistance, love and volunteered effort, comradeship and a listening ear, ideals and working hands. Laziness, selfishness, and fear can keep us from becoming involved when our help is needed.

My voice matters. I'll make myself heard

I realize trying to hold tight control of my life is impossible and stupid—but it's so hard to let go.

It's also hard not to let go. Which do we want? The difficulty of the task is not the issue. The real question is: Which is best? Which is more realistic?

It's true that the more we let go of control and rigidity, the better our physical health is apt to be, the better our mental health will be, and the better our spiritual health will be. And the better our relationship to life and the planet will be.

It's not terribly hard to let go. Sure, it will be difficult if we succumb to doom-like fears, tighten our bodies to the breaking point, shoot up our blood pressure, and treat the entire project as if it were World War III. The secret is to let go by letting go. It falls into place. There's a bonus. We've managed to relinquish an element of our life that blocked us, creating harm and alarm.

Today, I'll drop the reins for a while. I'll find out where my life wants to go.

If you won't hurt me, I won't hurt you.

BORIS PASTERNAK

A bond of trust is vitally important in any kind of relationship. There must be ground rules. A covenant is based on mutual dialogue instead of an authoritarian or ego-centered monologue.

None of us wants to be hurt in a relationship. Yet people hurt each other all the time, often inadvertently. This can be due to ignorance of someone else's feelings, or a blatant refusal to be caring, or an instinctive fear of being vulnerable. A lack of sensitivity stands in the way of intimacy.

It wouldn't be a bad idea in virtually any relationship to declare up front: "If you won't hurt me, I won't hurt you." It could be seen as a peacekeeping plan, a statement of tender purpose. It acknowledges a deep truth that we really don't, any of us, want to hurt or be hurt.

I'll do no harm. I'll respect the truth. It will come back to me.

JANUARY 23

I try hard to be happy. I work at it. But I'm not happy. What is the secret of being happy?

Don't try too hard. Happiness is elusive, like sunbeams in the morning or sea waves at the shore. We cannot grab hold of it, lock it up, and save it for a rainy day.

There are certain things we can do, however, to summon happiness into our lives. Stay hopeful. Emphasize positive factors and possibilities. Relate to other people honestly and openly. Seek help to uncover our own wounds and heal them. Maintain a sense of humor. Set new goals and do hard work to bring them alive. Recognize that we have bodies, minds, and souls. Try to balance them and integrate them into wholeness.

Be as practical, hard-nosed, and systematic about achieving happiness as you possibly can. Read how-to books. Attend classes. Go to workshops. Keep a journal. Finally, put your trust in serendipity, earth's occasional magic, chance, life's energy, and holy grace.

Today, I'll stop *trying,* and start *being.*

Now I realize that, although I never went much to school or received a diploma, I have kept right on learning.

LILLIAN GISH

Living is learning. However, many people seem not to learn. Why?

For one thing, we need to understand and admit failure when it comes—then place it behind us. It's essential to learn from failure. Transcend it. Let it teach us. It's awful to repeat the same mistakes forever! Instead we should set out courageously on new paths and be open to the transforming power of change.

Learning is free. There is no tuition. Classes are open to all of us. We teach each other, so instructor and student roles are constantly shifting. Honesty is the rule in life's classes. There is necessarily an absence of pretense, false values, and lies. There cannot be a diploma because the learning process never ends. The world remains our classroom.

If I'm learning, I'm still growing. Today, I'll open my mind to something new.

Why can't a child return to a parent even a bit of the love that has been poured out unselfishly and at great sacrifice?

Love is hard to measure. At times our human roles get in the way. In the place of a human being we perceive only a certain role: mother, father, daughter, son, wife, husband, or grandparent.

It's necessary to see a flesh-and-blood person beneath each role. One reason we don't is that roles themselves create all sorts of expectations. Why did my mother act that way and embarrass me? Why did my father cut the ground out from under me when I needed his understanding and support? How could my daughter have betrayed me by doing that? How can I ever forgive my son after what he did to me? My granddaughter had no right to criticize me. When I needed my granddad to be warm and loving, he was judgmental and cold.

All the above reactions stem from role expectations. All of us need to free ourselves, and other people deeply connected to our lives, from mere role playing. It is essential to be as honest as possible about our real identities, our feelings and motives, our real expectations, our real possibilities.

Today, I'll give everyone a clean slate. I'll look beyond what's owed or expected. I'll start with my love, and go from there

When something rotten like this happens.
Then you have your choice. You start to really
be alive, or you start to die. That's all.

JAMES AGEE

It's what we do with what happens to us that matters.
This is especially true of painful, threatening, or rotten
events that can bruise or defeat us.

We need to ask: Shall we let our emotions be bludgeoned to a bloody pulp or can we gain the strength to
learn invaluable lessons and go on living—even triumphantly? To grasp strength is vital. It can come from
one's personal faith, the strength of a close friend, the example of a role model, or simply an adamant refusal to
become dehumanized. From a position of strength we
continue to grow stronger.

Living and dying alike beckon to us in situations of
crisis. The decision is ours. If we want to start to really
be alive, this is a life-changing decision with vast repercussions. We will never again be the same as we were before.

Today, I'll try looking past bad luck and grievances.
I'll take a deep breath, and plan for better days.

Be a good friend. When you have a good day get on the phone and make plans. Don't cancel them. Value your plans. Remember, to have good friends you must be a good friend.

Friends are the staples of life. We should make vows to friends, cherish them, offer thanks for them.

But we often treat friends cavalierly, taking them for granted. We take, take, take while failing to give. We expect friends to be there for us in moments of need, while we may fail to be present for them at similar times. Sometimes we exaggerate our friends' faults and blemishes, while we adamantly refuse to extol their virtues or offer them praises.

I suppose the reason is that we're so close to real friends that we treat them as we might old shoes. They're here, reliable, tested, comfortable, and faithful. So we're not necessarily on our best behavior with them as we would be with party guests. We're sure they'll understand, without explanation.

We're better friends when we treat our friends better.

Today, I'll think about the people I love, and why. I'll pick up the phone or write a letter, now, and tell them so.

When I take off my glasses, especially on rainy nights, I get a far more beautiful view of the world than twenty-twenty people get.

RICHARD AVEDON

We've got to be able to see what's really there and not be limited by mere appearances.

If nothing else, age should teach us that true beauty may have little or nothing to do with a pretty or handsome appearance. How do we look at a building or house on a street? What if it is very old? Do we see it as a ramshackle place in disrepair? If so, we may miss its truth. It may possess great character, have a proud history, and still show an indomitable face to the world. This could be lost in a blur if we merely glanced at the house.

Most of us move through life too quickly, not stopping for second glances. There are far more beautiful views of the world available than those that twenty-twenty people get!

Today, I'm going to take off my glasses—and look.

I realize that I am not going to live forever. Can I handle this?

You'd better. Maybe sooner rather than later.

Of course there is widespread and deep belief in numerous religions and spiritual beliefs that the soul, or personality, continues after the death of the body.

But at this moment let's deal simply with the here and now. Yes, a lot of people fear death. Yet it seems a logical, clean-cut climax to our earthly existence. It's hard for most of us to spend a great deal of time on death because we're here, alive, living, struggling with life's joys and issues, problems and possibilities. It seems necessary to concentrate on the next immediate steps of this life instead of speculating about what comes afterward. At the same time, we've got to be prepared for the end of our lives—make our wishes known concerning our possessions, remember loved ones and friends, and develop a state of mind that contains readiness for our inevitable demise. Live fully—but leave some space for what is to come.

I'll recognize the inevitability of an ending—consider what's necessary—and then stride straight ahead into the future.

One of my two grown daughters is a lesbian, and lives with another woman; the other's in prison. I simply told them they'd both made some bad choices. Now only my daughter in prison will write to me.

One of the saddest things in the world is isolating ourselves from those who won't let us run their lives for them.

When we demand the right to control others' lives on our own terms, we are practicing conditional love. But there isn't any such thing. It's a contradiction. True love is unconditional. It contains no conditional clauses.

If we try to love, but also wish to dictate the terms of another person's life, we've embarked on an impossible situation. It's a bit like trying to be an absolute monarch, an old-fashioned king or queen, in a democratic society. To love means to trust. Anyone who's truly loved knows he or she is trusted with life. There is a deep awareness that love will never be withheld under any circumstances.

If I love, why must I judge? Today, I'll embrace those I care about. I'll try accepting without condition.

I'm single and older, have a good job, and have taken on many interests. But hey, life without that special person is very, very difficult.

Yearning for companionship is one of the most natural things in the world. But many people are single. Some always were, others are widows and widowers, still others are divorced. Ironically, a lot of people in relationships yearn to be singles.

Is the grass always greener on the other side? The answer seems to be that, regardless of whether we are with someone else or alone, we need to find ways that lead to self-fulfillment. A book entitled *The Lonely Crowd* explored how being with other people does not always seem to provide a solution. For the vast majority of us, no one person can ever bring total fulfillment into our lives.

Taking this a step further, the poet Marianne Moore pointed out that the cure for loneliness is solitude. We have to deal with ourselves. We must learn how to be alone, handle the demons, and find peace. Staying busy or becoming dependent upon someone else will not provide it.

I'm going to get used to being with myself, even when I'm also with others.

Poor Clifton, on the other hand, is still, after two months, wailing and sobbing over Maybelle's death. As she was well over ninety, gaga, and had driven him mad for years, this seems excessive and over-indulgent.

NOËL COWARD

People can be quite intolerant of how others feel.

Maybe there's even more intolerance of how feelings are expressed. We say it's all right for people to cry on occasion in public—but please, observe definite limits and good taste, and don't be melodramatic.

After two partners break up, ending a relationship or marriage, their friends will gladly put up with a bit of expected grieving. Before long, however, either grief takes its leave or else a sad-faced friend is given the sack. The same scenario is often played out after a death. What is described as a decent period of mourning is expected to segue into restored mirth. But everyone needs to grieve in their own time, and we need to treat our friends with sensitivity and care when they're mourning or hurting, hoping they'll return the favor when our turn to grieve comes.

I'll be open to other people's true feelings, with no lies and no masks.

I have learned to take pain in small segments.
I will get through the next half-hour. Then,
the next.

There's only so much we can take at a time. When we attempt to look out over the vast span of our lives, we are mystified, immobilized.

Yet if we can differentiate between portions of the immense vista of life, and endeavor to cope only with a workable part of it, perhaps we can manage effectively. Pain is unlike anything else. It makes extraordinary demands on us. Too, it becomes familiar. We grow accustomed to when it comes, when it goes. Imagining and anticipating a full span of uninterrupted pain can be devastating. We need to yield and deal pragmatically with pain on our own terms in whatever ways we can.

Life itself is a bit like pain in this regard. We can't take it in one fell swoop, nor are we asked to. Yet, in segments, we find that we gradually learn how to manage it when its sharp sensations are balanced by quiet nurturing, its pains with celebrations of joy.

I won't look at life simply as a whole, but as a wonderful collection of fragments.

The old days? What old days? I don't remember a thing. What do the old days matter when there's today to live?

RODNEY HALL

It's tragic to see someone obsessed with frantic absorption in the present moment, like a moth darting into a hot flame. Often this person remains oblivious to the past—its mistakes and glories alike—as a hinge of meaning for the present.

Old days are a permanent part of our lives. We remember some as good, others bad. Always they are our teachers. We can recognize ourselves in them as if they were mirrors. Our mothers and fathers are basic leading characters in our old days, along with siblings, grandparents, childhood friends, and certain authority figures at school. A few ghosts and shadow figures of our childhood we remember dimly, although they can be vivid when we dream. Leave room in memory for beloved pets, fascinating places we visited, experiences in school, embarrassing failures (did anyone notice?), and breakthrough experiences when we grew by leaps and bounds.

Take time to remember the old days, forgiving what we can, celebrating what we may, and always learning from them.

I'm going to hold onto my memories, the good and bad, the easy and difficult, and never, never forget them.

I try to giggle thirteen times a day. Sounds hard but gradually it becomes so foolish, it's fun. Cost? None.

We need to bring fun into life. Just simple, ridiculous, belly-laughing fun. Are we afraid of fun? Does it embarrass us? Maybe it seems foolishly childish to us very, very serious grown-ups! How many years have we struggled to keep a straight face?

Giggling thirteen times a day might be a good start. We could follow that by learning how to laugh at pomposity, howl at phoniness. Potential scenarios are limitless.

A great gift as we grow older is to become mellower, laugh more gently and often, and gaze openly at the emperor parading without clothes. It's been said that in the divine comedy, God must have a wonderful sense of humor. Why? Because God created us.

With all of life's manifold struggles and problems, it behooves us to practice the art of laughter. Let's have fun. Let's place things in perspective and never be afraid of looking foolish.

I'm going to enjoy what's ridiculous and not let anyone ever take it away from me.

FEBRUARY 5

I did not retire! "Retire" is something insurance-company executives do, with golf carts—not what I did.

MARCIA DAVENPORT

Retirement has many different faces. For some it is a splendid adventure. For others it is a mistake and a cause of sadness.

It shouldn't mean giving up. It's not meant to be a form of dying. In fact, it can be an opportunity to change pace and direction, to continue to grow and develop as a person, to do things one was not previously able to do and have more time to expand one's horizons.

Good retirement requires planning, common sense, a leap of faith, and the awareness that one is starting out upon a new journey. It can also mean ending an old life pattern that became a treadmill and something of a bore, bringing few surprises. To retire creatively is to seek fresh surprises. It's an opportunity to delve into new byways and paths of life, choosing unexpected turns in the road. At its best it's a journey deep into self and the meaning of life.

I'll change "retire" to "go forward," and I'll do it with zest and courage.

Let the past go. Be forgiving. Remember that nobody is perfect.

Why is this so hard for us to do most of the time? We tend to hug the past as if it were a lover, even when it has caused us untold pain and distress. Why don't we let go of it and live in the present moment? We can keep our memories without letting them control us.

It seems even harder for us to forgive past hurts, real or imaginary betrayals, transgressions, and broken dreams. Sometimes we hold onto an old grudge as if it were a sacred object. We relive an old argument over and over again in our thoughts, summoning it to a position of honor in our mind, playing it over as we would an old video.

The victim of all this is ourselves. We deny our own peace. We permit anger to burst into a hot flame inside us. We keep blaming someone else. Yet we are no more perfect than that hapless person locked in our past. When we are able to forgive him or her, we make a big contribution to our own peace. Our healing begins.

Today, I'll forgive what I had thought was unforgivable. I'll stop punishing myself.

People refused to listen, to understand,
to share.

ELIE WIESEL

People often do not want to see what is right before their eyes in terms of human pain.

Many of us lived through the years of the Holocaust, with its death and destruction. We have experienced firsthand the evils of racism and sexism. Wars, refugees, starvation, and denial are a part of the legacy of our time. In the midst of such tragedy, a shocking number of people have chosen not to see, hear, or speak.

We are bound closely together in our human experience. It is extremely important for all of us to draw closer together in an awareness of shared life. This includes the younger and the older. We can't ever look at one another as strangers who are out-of-touch, don't understand, or are some kind of freaks. We must not refuse to listen to one another—and to hear. We must not refuse to understand one another—and to show empathy. We must not refuse to share with one another—and to be friends.

I'll open up my eyes, my ears, my hands, my entire life, and quit playing dead.

FEBRUARY 8

You live only once, and for this one time you live a temporary life, in the vain hope that one day real life will begin. That's how we exist.

IGNAZIO SILONE

How could we avoid real life—birth, death, love, work, mystery? Real life is all around us and within us.

But let's face it, some of us treat it as temporary from time to time: when we avoid decisions that are necessary for our fulfillment; when we put off until tomorrow what crucially needs to be done today; when we tell lies to ourselves and others about what really matters; when we deny hope.

Aging confronts us with the truth that we exist on the edge of infinite possibilities, yet we do not have all the time in the world to waste. It's absolutely necessary to see that real life is now, in this instant—and to act upon it.

I choose to be a real person who lives a real life.

I keep asking myself if I have anything left to strive for.

It is so easy to give up. It can become a long, drawn-out process of denying hope and elevating low self-esteem to an art.

We should never measure ourselves against the world's images of success. In fact, much imagery of that kind is sheer fabrication. The world's greatest movie star may be an emotional disaster while an unknown clerk is an enormous success at the business of living. Each of us is unique, possessing creation's inner beauty and a startling capacity for life.

What is left to strive for? Here are a few things. Love in a world filled with too much hatred. Honesty in small things as well as big ones. Justice in human situations that flagrantly deny it. Joy in place of despair. Courage to change what needs to be changed. Laughter to ease pain. Beauty to illuminate the soul. Compassion to outlaw cruelty. Patience to survive with grace. It's clear that all of us need to strive all the time for what is better, brighter, and lifts up life to its full potential.

I'll look for things to awaken my soul. I'll see the wonder of living.

Don't moan. Don't complain. Think positively.

KATHARINE HEPBURN

It seems easy to moan, but isn't. It opens up a Pandora's box of conflicting and negative feelings that get in the way of either offering thanks for life or just celebrating its virtues.

Of course, to complain is to deny growth and remain an infant emotionally. It doesn't require much stamina to complain. To think positively, on the other hand, is to take a big step forward. It means owning up to one's place in the universe—claiming it, wanting it, being prepared to work and sacrifice for it.

Positive thinking can be like oxygen for older, more mature people who have learned its benefits well. It is life-giving. It illuminates the soul. It stirs the mind to action.

I'll think twice when I start to complain. I'll try thinking instead of the things I'm grateful for.

How can I deal honestly with my life as it is, not as I wish it were?

The best way? Open our eyes wide, look around and see what's there, take a deep breath, and dive decisively into the center of life as if it were a deep pool of water.

Simple? Yes and no. Unquestionably, it can be done. But many people refuse. You see, it requires giving up mere wishing. It demands that we acknowledge what is clearly before our very eyes.

Growing older, we are foolish to choose dishonesty over honesty about life. Now our decisions take on a literal survival meaning. They can define the remainder of our life on earth and also our eternal goals of the spirit. They are extraordinarily powerful. We hold this power in our hands.

I'm going to look life squarely in the eye.

For to take that other way would mean that I should lose myself. I should no longer be a person.

CHRISTOPHER ISHERWOOD

We can't let anyone try to take away our truth, our reality. Yet people are waiting in the wings all the time to do precisely that.

Some of them want to make us conform to their definition of what is correct behavior or a desirable style of life. If we bend to their wishes, they imply that henceforward they will leave us alone. But the price is too high. It kills a vital part of us, and threatens our whole self.

Even after requiring us to make such a sacrifice, however, these same people will not leave us alone. Their cookie cutters will always be at work on us, shaping us into ever new and acceptable forms alien to our very selves.

We've got to realize, all of us, how essential it is for us to become and remain our true selves. We can't let anybody interfere with our humanity, our rights, our freedom, our personhood.

Today, I'll take myself as I am. I'll celebrate myself.

FEBRUARY 13

Too much of a good thing can be wonderful.

MAE WEST

Why do we tend to feel guilty when we're having a good time? Why do we place harshly puritanical judgments on pleasure and fun? At times there seems to be a vestigial need to do this.

Supposedly we older people have matured to the point where we have put away silly hangups. Long ago we should have learned how to deal constructively with guilt—and how to be aware we've earned the right to release and fulfillment, laughter and fun. Why should we give a tinker's damn anymore about that old saw "what other people think"?

Moderation is no longer a particularly useful axiom for us. Why? Because we engage in moderation by default. The truth is that life dictates its necessity for us. It's time to balance our long, long term of obedience to the work ethic with the new thrill of letting ourselves be open to a chance for happiness.

Today, I declare my independence.

FEBRUARY 14

I am invisible, understand, simply because
people refuse to see me.

RALPH ELLISON

Some people simply refuse to see anyone who is different. So they end up looking at a stereotype instead.

There are many older men and women whom others
refuse to see for a variety of reasons. First, worshipers of a
youth cult are disturbed and turned off by the presence
of anyone aging. It's a reminder of their own future, and
they wish to block it out. Second, older people may
move more slowly, need to walk with a cane, or find it
difficult to stand waiting in a long line. This indicates a
human need, and there are people who don't wish to be
bothered by dealing with human need. Third, seniors do
not fit a stereotype of "average"; they are "different" from
the accepted norm.

Hence, we can become invisible to the naked eye.

I'll refuse to be invisible, ever.

My husband died eight months ago. I can't accept the fact that he's not coming back. I can't live without him. He was everything to me. I cry all the time. I cry when I go to bed and reach out and there is only a pillow there.

Grief is a natural reaction to loss. It is healthy to grieve, to grant expression to feelings, and let go of a rigid, stoical control.

However, there comes a time when grief should run its course. Life beckons to us once again. Other people need our time and attention. The loved one who has died undoubtedly wants us to experience the richness and fullness of life, not stay imprisoned in sadness.

It is not an act of disloyalty to a departed loved one to start life anew. It is an act of deep loyalty precisely because it is an act of living. A loved one who has departed does not want us to embrace death prematurely, or turn our back on living, or exist inside a mausoleum. Let life come.

I'll cry when I must, and then I'll stop, open my eyes, and start looking for new possibilities.

Was this what it came to—that you could never escape?

ANNE TYLER

We have to believe that we can make changes in our lives. Otherwise we become victims.

Possessing the power to make changes, however, does not in any way free us from the need to confront life's demands. We can't rub a genie's lamp, make three wishes, and have them magically granted. It's necessary to work our way through problems. The point is: We can make the fastest progress by expeditiously tackling the rough terrain one step at a time.

The really hard question is: Is there escape from aging? No—but there is escape from negative thinking about it. We can be grateful for the positive gifts of growing more mature, finally coming to see the whole of life in perspective, and reaching a coveted and golden place of wisdom.

I'll focus today on gratitude. I'm grateful for change, and the chance for something new.

If I knew that I had just five months to live, what would I want to do?

It is a classic question for all of us. Some would choose travel to places they had always yearned to visit. Others might stay home and get life's affairs in order, or finish a significant piece of creative work, maybe meditate in a quiet place and go fishing.

Most of us would probably want to appreciate life for the last time—savor its richness, honor its simplicity, marvel at its intricate complexity. We'd have reached a precious moment to hear a favorite selection of music for the last time, read a beloved poem or book, dine on a cherished dish, or swim off a treasured beach.

Yet we can do these things now. We don't have to wait until we have just five months to live.

What would I do today if it were my last? I'll try living each day thus.

Hell—not fiery and romantic but grey, greasy, dismal—is just around the corner.

J. B. PRIESTLEY

Hell on earth is a major human invention. It raises hard questions: Why do we ever choose to pursue unhappiness, cater to our own worst instincts, or bar with determination the least glimmer of joy in our lives?

As we grow older we accumulate more practice in dealing with hell on earth. Most of us have visited this territory on more than one occasion. So we're familiar with its hotels and restaurants, travel agents and beaches, hills and valleys. We know hell on earth from our own experience. This is precisely why we need to reject it with an adamant *No!* From firsthand knowledge we're aware that it's shabby, sullied, shoddy, smudged, sordid, and slimy. Who in one's right mind would wish to stay there?

Discernment is a gift of maturity. One way we can exercise discernment is to see through the illusion of fascination that mistakenly surrounds hell on earth. It isn't fascinating at all. It's a bloody bore.

I won't play a part in creating my own hell. I'll resist it with every fiber of my being.

FEBRUARY 19

If people allow themselves a chance to get involved in something other than their disappointments, they can loosen the death grip they keep on their agony.

Who wants agony? Probably none of us. Yet a number of us remain locked inside it.

Disappointments can multiply, especially if we're counting. They seem to feed on one another. Then we get to a place where we expect to be disappointed. This sets in motion a lot of negative energy. The best solution is to focus on the opposite of disappointments: new changes, new opportunities. They exist. We block their view, especially if our focus does not include their possibility. If we have already decided we're going to be disappointed again—again and again—we make it virtually impossible for fresh ideas to come into our line of vision, let alone be dealt with in positive ways.

Try to realize: Life is life—we're alive! Life always means anything can happen to us, including unexpected, good, and even revolutionary things.

Today I'll try exerting positive energy in every aspect of my life. I'll meet the world anew.

FEBRUARY 20

Could she have wished to be trodden down in a riot, be a mark for anger, or go down on a helpless abandoned ship?

ELIZABETH BOWEN

Our lives sometimes fall into ruts. We plod along bored and unfulfilled, while other people mistakenly believe we like our condition and are happy.

What a mess. Our reaction can be extreme. At certain times we rebel suddenly, go overboard by embracing anything to reverse the course. A better approach is to decide upon an alternative course of living and move at a steady, even pace toward implementing it. This means being honest about what we want; letting our feelings be known to others; generating energy for change instead of remaining passive, bored, and unproductive.

While the sensation of drastic change may appear a lively antidote for sameness, remember that it's not a great pleasure to be trodden down in a riot. Nor is there much joy when one is a mark for violent anger. Going down on a helpless abandoned ship offers no lasting thrill. As we grow in maturity, let's seek more lasting and constructive alternatives to shake up our lives.

I'll allow room for my fantasies—but I'll root them in reality

FEBRUARY 21

This moment is of supreme importance. In another moment it will be gone. Can I hold onto it?

No. We cannot place time inside a jar as if it were honey. Time is like the air. It brushes against our face and is gone forever.

It is important that we honor each moment as it comes. Acknowledge it fully. Take delight in it as we may. Recognize the sacred quality of time, its transient nature, its extraordinary beauty as a sheer gift.

Almost as soon as it came, the moment is gone, replaced with another one. The moments multiply and make an hour, a day, a week, a month, a year, a life. We can learn the art of gracefully letting a moment go when it is ready, offering thanks for it, anticipating its successor. This means being open to the precious gift of the moment, realizing its import. While seasons return, moments do not.

I won't cling to the moment. I'll set it free—making room for the next one.

People think it's morbid to read the obituaries. Wait'll they lose a mate. I read them every day, looking for men who died at the same age as Rob. I *have* to read them. Now that I know about grief, I can't seem to ignore it.

The best newspapers print wonderful obituaries filled with highlights of a person's life, colorful details, occasional anecdotes, and a true sense of personality and character. It is a final homage, a public appreciation, a celebration of the incredible uniqueness of a particular human being.

Someday people may read our obituary. It's not morbid at all to read obituaries. Quite the contrary. They're indispensable accounts concerning the passage of life. They're stories that help to provide a chronicle of time.

It's time we were all more honest about obituaries. Reading them represents the opposite of denial of grief and death. When we know about grief and have survived it, an obituary is a life connection for us. Encountering someone else's past, we may acknowledge our own passing that is in progress. We can honestly mourn someone whom we have loved, and make our mourning positive by celebrating the life with joy and gratitude.

Today, I'll think about the passing of lives. I'll look for the connections—and celebrate, honor, and renew my commitments.

Realization dawned on me that no one else is going to solve my problems. I have to. Underneath years of unhappiness I discovered myself as a new person whose life is worthwhile.

One of the worst exercises in futility is to wait for someone else to come along like Galahad and rescue us while we languish in frustration and weakness, feel victimized, and lack the courage or strength to make a decision.

Yet we must. The beginning of wisdom is the realization that no one else can do this for us. When we refuse to realize it, we remain indecisive, looking perpetually to left and right, but not moving forward. This creates great unhappiness not only for ourselves, but also for other people who are connected to our lives, and can lead to extremely serious problems at home, in our relationships, at work, within our minds and souls; and beyond these, in our expectations or sense of failure, or use of money, and the very direction our lives are taking.

Self-discovery as a worthwhile person is an extremely positive experience. A key is required, however. The key is our individual initiative. This grows out of our awareness that no one else can live our life for us.

Today, I'll take the wheel. I'll try taking responsibility for my own life. I'll set out to discover where that may lead.

FEBRUARY 24

As I love myself, so will I love my neighbor.

SAM KEEN

Sometimes we forget to love ourselves. This isn't unselfish at all; actually it is a form of murder. Who gets killed? We do.

All of us grew up with what were known as the two Great Commandments: love God, and love your neighbor. This noticeably left out love of self. The original biblical quotation was "Love your neighbor as yourself" and unless we have a healthy love of self, we can't manage to obey those two commandments at all. If we don't love ourselves we don't possess love. Under these circumstances, we project a kind of phony love outward to other people. Often we end up harming them because, instead of loving, we simply meet needs of our own by making an appearance of doing good.

When we love ourselves in a mature and healthy way, however, we can give love to others.

Today, I'll start small. I'll treat myself with love.

FEBRUARY 25

Loneliness is terrifying. I leave a light burning all night in a small room adjoining my bedroom, but still I awaken scared to death and my loneliness is overwhelming.

Keep the light burning. Loneliness is understandable. We need to handle it the best way we can.

We can also ask the questions: Why am I suffering such an overwhelming sense of loneliness? Do I miss terribly a spouse or loved one who has died? Is aging, for example, deeply threatening to me? Am I confronting the idea of my own mortality? What scares me?

Learning how to be by oneself—yet not feel acutely alone—is a great gift. Some find companionship in books, others in music or a garden; still more cherish pets, friends who are nearby, pen pals, activities that carry them outside their immediate environment for a certain amount of time. All of us need to seek and find the companionship we need.

I'll make myself open to all the companionship and community surrounding me in this life.

What matters is not whether life loves us, but that we love life.

CHARLOTTE SALOMON

Life can be a fickle lover, tossing us over for someone else, betraying us with an easy smile, and tearing up our security as if it were a piece of paper. We all know that life provides us with ups and downs, happy sunrises and dark blues. Anyone who's been around the block knows life cannot be depended on. Ever.

So? Do we allow this fact to make us bitter, sour, and a bundle of rage? If we do, we're our own worst enemy. Life, despite its mercurial qualities, remains the most beautiful gift. It is our very space.

What happens when we love life? We also love trees, flowers, streams, oceans, mountains, hills, valleys, dogs, cats, birds, fishes, music, books, sun, moon, stars, water, wine, bread—and people.

I'll make myself a lover.

FEBRUARY 27

The clock is ticking the minutes away. My minutes. Each tick synchronizes with a heartbeat.

SAM KEEN

It seems that we are either oblivious to our mortality or else obsessed by it. Let's try to find a middle ground between the two.

One extreme view posits the question: Why worry about tomorrow? It suggests that we have all the time in the world: Time itself is limitless, opportunity unrestricted, death a mere mirage.

Yet the clock is ticking. So is our heart. We have only so much time to do so many things. We need to view time as a friend, not an enemy. It reminds us that it is limited. This awakens us to a vast area of possibilities and choices. It makes us come alive. Time places all of life within a context. We can choose how we wish to live: the boundaries that we want to set; the goals that appear to be reasonable; the style that fits our personality.

I'll listen to the heartbeat of life. I'll respond by living fully.

FEBRUARY 28

If we cannot agree, let us at any rate agree to differ, but let us part as friends.

MOHAMMAD ALI JINNAH

As we mature, and some of us even approach the end of our lives, the time has come to make peace with those who differ from us, including supposed enemies.

It is utterly tragic to observe stubborn people who refuse to forgive past wrongs and perpetuate the endless small civil wars of this world. These are the worst kind of wars, especially within families. Yet maturity signifies a respect for friendship as well as a propensity for it. Why be enemies? Why participate in the destructive and self-destructive exercise of enmity?

Unfortunately, enmity is legion and can be found in such diverse places as the bitterness of a divorce, rage rooted in an old business deal that went wrong, and a sullen refusal to forgive a parent or a child. Enough! More friends are needed, not enemies.

I resolve to be a peacemaker and a friend. Where forgiveness can heal, I will forgive.

All my life I've been sick and tired. Now I'm sick and tired of being sick and tired.

FANNIE LOU HAMER

These famous lines stirred a generation. They were heard as a clarion call to human freedom. Their meaning is universal. They are timeless.

All of us feel sick and tired in very serious ways from time to time. Perhaps it is a matter of health, a flawed relationship, a bad job, a family crisis, financial worry, or a personal fantasy of ours at war with reality—or the car breaks down. As our situation worsens we grow sick and tired of it. What to do? There has to be a big change. A fundamental change. It needs to occur now rather than later.

The message is: Get on with it. Change the situation that is making us sick and tired. Don't put off to tomorrow what we are able to do about it today. This is one of those moments when it is time to start turning our life around.

I'm ready for change. I won't delay another moment.

MARCH 1

It's hard to imagine, but once I dreaded turning thirty. Now that AIDS has taken so many of my friends, forty looks very sweet—fifty, a promised land.

In World War I the flowering of a generation of youth was cut down in the trenches of Europe.

AIDS is now ruthlessly killing another generation. A result of this is a completely different view of death. A natural lifespan is being denied millions of people. So, life's meaning has to be expressed in far more immediate terms than before.

Where there is no tomorrow, today takes on a deeper significance. We can no longer put off to tomorrow what needs to be done now. Life is measured more in terms of quality than quantity. This brings the generations closer, for many young people grow accustomed to looking death in the face at thirty or forty, not simply at seventy or eighty. As life's meaning becomes compressed into fewer years, many of our attitudes and beliefs are changing.

I'm going to meet today—this hour, this moment—exactly as I feel. I won't be bound by a label or a number.

MARCH 2

Some say a cup of camomile tea or a warm bath can induce relaxation, but gratitude is the great wooer of sleep.

ELIZABETH YATES

Have you ever tossed and tossed, this way and that way, while relaxation eluded you with the agility of mercury?

There are timeworn remedies, including a cup of camomile tea and a warm bath. Of course, peace of mind never hurts, either. But still, there are nights when apparently nothing is going to help very much. Days, too, when relaxation seems as evasive as honesty in politics.

We are wound up like old-fashioned clocks. First, an excruciating problem presents itself to our already weary consciousness; then, an unsolvable dilemma returns in full fury, dismaying us, catching us off balance, draining us of joy and energy. The best thing to do? Quit wrestling with such unhappy ghosts and turn elsewhere. Look at what is positive about our life. Express gratitude for one more moment to be alive. Try to share the miracle of living. Embrace the gift of wholeness.

Today, I'll turn my back on anxiety and hopelessness. Life is full of beauty, and I'm grateful to be a part of it.

MARCH 3

Most of us seniors are sharp as a tack and can run circles around eighteen-year-olds who think they're ultrasmart when actually they are wet behind the ears.

I find human beings are miracles. They amaze me. I love the wisdom and maturity of age, and also the drive and spunk of youth. There is, thank God, room for both.

Some seniors, I must say, are not sharp as a tack, while some youths cannot be described as wet behind the ears. Generalities are not helpful here. What matters is being able to see each other as we are. This includes perceiving the gifts and skills, the faults and limitations, of each.

Ironically, there are some seniors who are characterized by spunk and drive instead of maturity and wisdom. At the same time, some youths are in fact old souls. Their wisdom and maturity are known to all in their family and school settings. If they lack anything, it's spunk and drive. The solution? Let's try for well-rounded lives seasoned by all the good spices we can get.

I'm full of spunk and wisdom. I'll strive to balance them.

The friends got up to pay the bill. They were such old friends they didn't even grab for each other's checks.

ELLEN CONLEY

Aren't old friends wonderful? Yes. There is a warm camaraderie, an absence of phoniness, a directness that we often find lacking with acquaintances and strangers.

Friends are particularly important in our lives as we grow older. We lose some of them by geographical separation or death. For those remaining, friendship becomes a sacrament with deep meaning.

We love old, good friends. Love. This carries with it a curious corollary: There are definite moments when we don't like them too much. The same thing has happened with members of our biological family. We can become outraged at them, often over a seemingly small matter. This is related to the fact that the worst wars are civil wars. Domestic wars within families are civil wars. But we continue to love even as we announce hate. At such a moment, we don't like; but we continue to love. Blood is thicker than water. Old friends are family, too. Concentrate on loving them. Strive to like them, even in difficult moments. They are rare creatures.

Friendship is a full-time occupation. Today, I'll take my work seriously.

To live alone is better than making a bad choice and suffering the consequences. I have seen friends suffer untold misery with someone unsuitable, unsupportive, and unstable.

Some people sadly seem to live alone in an unrewarding relationship. Yet others who actually live by themselves seem happily involved with all kinds of wonderful people in a myriad of situations.

We're all so different. Universal prescriptions for happiness cannot be handed out over the counter. For some people, to live alone is the best thing to do; they find fulfillment in life without a close partner. For others, to live alone is fatal; a relationship is a necessity.

We need to figure out exactly what kind of person we are. If we're better off alone, let's try to have the courage and insight to make a creative life based on that truth and avoid the torture chamber of a doomed relationship. However, if we're better off living in a relationship with someone else, let's try to find someone who fills the bill. Above all, let's grow up—at whatever age.

Today, I'll think about who I am and what it is I want. I'll prepare to be surprised.

When there's nothing you can do about anything, do everything you can.

JAMES BROUGHTON

This is one of the greatest secrets of all time. A great many people, however, when confronted with nothing to do, simply stop. They give up. They surrender the palace. They go away into unhappy exile. They're fools.

At precisely the same moment when there is apparently nothing we can do about anything, that's the time to move into action. Devise a strategy. Make a plan. Call a meeting. Adopt Plan B. Find an alternative.

Faced with the need to surrender, there is always far more to do than we give ourselves credit for. It is the moment to lift up our spirit and adamantly refuse to be defeated. It is the moment to stir up our mind and suddenly become creative, especially if we have just about run out of creativity. It is the moment to get our body moving and fight laziness. It is the moment to take a full breath of fresh air, leap up, and decide to reverse direction. To pull chestnuts out of the fire. To do everything we can.

I'll do everything I can.

I will be sixty-nine years old. I have a boyfriend. He is going to be seventy-one. Our sex life is wonderful. For the first time in my life, and after years of a poor marriage, I've had orgasms and climaxes. We both feel like teenagers.

Teenagers might wish to feel so good. Isn't it great that you have found each other, with such happiness as well?

Society has foolishly held a reproving view of seniors as sexless. Or, at least that seniors should be sexless. This grows from a view of sex as intrinsically evil outside of conventional marriage. Rubbish!

Many seniors are widows or widowers. A number are divorced. Often their families like to assume they are dis-interested in sex, without libidinous desire. Love and sex are God-given gifts to human beings. Seniors wish to partake of them and participate fully in life. The puri-tanical, narrow, judgmental view that seniors should be sexless is an outrage against the human spirit. Stereotyp-ing seniors, it seeks to deprive older women and men of life, liberty, and the pursuit of happiness.

What's age-appropriate? Today, I'll let go and play.

MARCH 8

We neither love nor hurt because we do not try to reach each other.

EDWARD ALBEE

How tragic when this occurs. Indifference is far worse, far colder than what we call hate. Hate, at least, is filled with passion. It implies caring and love gone wrong. It may be open to remedy.

Indifference, however, is without caring. Other people are mere blurs instead of human beings. Human need becomes a bore. An indifferent person exists in a sort of vacuum, not seeing or feeling beyond minimal requirements to keep breathing. A huge, indifferent bureaucracy is the end result of such personal attitudes multiplied.

What should we try to do with our lives to escape such a curse? Reach each other! Reach out. Touch. Feel. Be fully aware of others. All this is very threatening to those people who, in Greta Garbo's famous words, want to be alone. But do they, really? Many who say they wish to be left alone are instead crying out for human communication, concern, and love. We must not be afraid to be alive.

I'll banish indifference from my life. I'll care and feel.

MARCH 9

I often wonder why we elderly folk are so stubborn and self-centered. Why can't we love our kids enough to give up our own desires and make it easier for all?

It is human nature to be stubborn and self-centered. It is love that opens us up to compromise, flexibility, and feeling a concern for others. Elderly people are no more or less stubborn and self-centered than anyone else.

When we feel ignored, neglected, and hurt, it's natural for us to become self-centered. Survival dictates that if no one else cares for us, we must make up for their lack of caring. If we don't, who will?

All of us have a right to our desires. Older women and men should not give up desires any more than anyone else. Compromise is desirable. It happens when any of us is able to fulfill our desires without standing in the way of others to do the same. But no one should ever be asked to bear a disproportionate burden to make it easier for someone else. Sometimes a lack of self-esteem makes us ready to give up our rights. Self-esteem is essential. Keep it up.

I'll compromise where it's desirable, but I'll hold to my desires.

When I see the hunger of a child, I see violence. Violence is the destruction of human beings—mentally, physically, or spiritually.

RODOLFO GONZALEZ

Violence is everywhere, all around us, and sometimes within us, too. The only way to stop violence is to become a nonviolent person, and try to create a nonviolent world.

Gandhi and Martin Luther King, Jr., are two strong people who incarnated the idea of nonviolence. Nonviolence is a way of life, not a political stratagem. Nonviolence is being practiced when a hungry child is fed; anyone who is abused is saved from it; an older man or woman living in impoverishment, abuse, and dire conditions is rescued and enabled to have a better life.

The point is: We must keep our own eyes open to see violence against human beings, wherever it may appear. The destruction of people's minds, bodies, and spirits is our concern, our responsibility. We cannot save the whole world, but we can save part of it—here and now.

I'll do all I can, on whatever scale, to stop violence.

MARCH 11

Most of us can do little about the situation in the Middle East or Central America, but there are many shut-ins who are alone and would love a friendly visit, a trip to the grocery store, or even a phone call.

There is so much we can do. It is selfish and self-defeating to sit on the sidelines and refuse to participate in life.

Some of us will want to concentrate on precisely what we can do about the situation in the Middle East or Central America or another part of the world whose problems matter a lot to us. We can organize around a particular issue, bring pressure to bear on politicians, raise funds, request the media to provide information, and help bring about needed change.

Others will wish to volunteer our time and effort closer to home. Here, human needs surround us. There is someone waiting to receive a friendly visit from a good listener. Someone who needs food. Someone who needs a ride. There is someone waiting who desperately needs contact with a human being who cares, wants to help, and is willing to be a friend.

I refuse to sit on the sidelines.

The joy of being older is that in one's life one can, towards the end of the run, over-act appallingly.

QUENTIN CRISP

Home free! Too many people, all their lives, are never free even to be themselves, let alone over-act.

Just to be able to become themselves would represent such a rich blessing. To walk outside a dark, dank closet of tragic self-containment. To say to the world, "Here I am!" To laugh and cry exuberantly and unashamedly with other people who laugh and cry.

Even better is the liberation to over-act, to be fully present in the great play that is life. Finally, we no longer need to soft-pedal the expression of our feelings. We may stride onstage in the bright fullness of light, belt our song, be outrageous if doing that fits our mood, and have an absolutely splendid time. This isn't simply a wonderful gift for us. It is the best present we can give to others: Ourselves, in full bloom.

I resolve to be myself, fully present, regardless of the world's expectations.

I told myself over many years that my life was empty without someone else in it. But *I'm* in it! My life is not empty at all. I'm grateful for its fullness.

Make your move! It's time. Dead ends are not very pleasurable or productive places to be. They are not springboards of hope, are they? It's good to trade them in for something better.

It's easy for us to construct a fantasy about needing a "someone" to make us happy. It is a cop-out. It relieves us of the responsibility to get to work creating our own happiness. All we need (we say) is for Mr. Right or Ms. Right to appear, the ideal figment of our imagination. According to the script, he or she will just walk into our life spontaneously, solve our problems, give us a rush of ecstasy and a glimpse of eternal joy, and we'll live happily ever after.

Oh. It isn't like that, is it? Sure, someone can hand us a gift of pleasure (usually laced with a bit of sadness, too) but no one else can make us happy. It's not up to anyone else. It's up to us.

Today, I'll think about what happiness means for me.

But one thing took root in me—the conviction that morality is the basis of things, and that truth is the substance of all morality. Truth became my sole objective.

MOHANDAS K. GANDHI

Truth is indispensable, yet many people fear it, oppose it, and live lives that are lies. Why do they?

At times financial expediency seems to dictate the answer. In other words, money is more important than anything else. Or, cowardice and defeatism assert themselves: What's the use? Or sometimes, a baffling inability to simply stand up and tell the truth, to let the chips fall where they may, takes over. Where is courage? Without truth, human relationships are frequently doomed, sadness is consummated, and untold lives are crippled permanently.

We need to tell the truth and ask for the truth from others. The best way to start is by telling the truth ourselves in daily ways that appear to be small and unthreatening. It can easily become a habit. When we realize that most people like it and appreciate it, we grow in confidence. Soon we find that we are able to tell the truth in more demanding situations. We possess the strength.

I respect the truth. I honor it. I'll go forward telling the truth.

Everyone is born with a creative spirit. Creating something can range from cutting out paper dolls to composing a great piece of music.

Creation is wonderful, isn't it? It takes many forms. Its impulse is life's energy. Creation keeps us alive, seeking ever new ways of expression.

One of the best things about creative energy is that we want to share with others what we have created. It's no fun sitting alone in a room surrounded by one's paintings, sketches, or sculpture. We want to invite others to see it, too. We need their criticism. It's important for us to know how others relate to our work and what meaning they find in it.

Some of us play a musical instrument or sing, others compose music. Some write poems, essays, or stories, while others speak lines. Always we should encourage other people to discover the sources of their own creative energy. We need them to help us discover our own. Creation isn't selfish. It means sharing.

When did I last make something totally new? When did I have the satisfaction of creating something from nothing? Today, I'll flex my talents—for others, for me.

While everything appears to live and die, it is only the appearance of things which lives and dies. The dead are buried. Their memory is not.

NOAH BENSHEA

Our memories are vast and deep as the ocean. We store virtually everything in our memories: hate and love, horror and beauty, numbness and forgiveness.

When we have loved, the people involved with us can never perish. They live on in our consciousness, our memory. Even when their bodies have undergone burial, our memory of them can never be buried. It keeps them alive in timeless orbit.

We remember. Vividly. Each detail. The past is present. Our childhood comes alive. Personalities in junior high school are as present as people we met last week. A loved one, long gone, smiles, laughs, embraces us. There is a raw immediacy linking the past to our present moment. The gusto is real. In fact, the present moment—the now—lacks true recognition without what went before it. The past validates it. In this sense, no one whom we have loved is dead. Our lovers and friends who are gone live in our memory, our recognition, our love in this present moment.

I'll keep my memories alive—seeding them with new ones.

In an exceptionally bright moment of truth I realized I was being treated as a thing instead of a person. How can I survive when impersonality leaps out at me?

We have to. Impersonality leaps out at most of us several times a day.

It is essential to know we are a person. This, when without warning somebody starts to treat us as a thing. What is a thing? An impersonal object. A body in somebody else's way. Someone whose feelings are denied. We are being treated as a thing when nobody cares. When we cry, and nobody listens. When we laugh, and nobody shares it. When people want to make money off us, but don't give a damn about us. When, instead of being appreciated as us, we are regarded simply as a burden, an obstacle, a problem, a number, a cipher.

The best way to deal with the problem is to turn it around. To listen when someone cries. To share someone's laughter. To appreciate another, endeavoring to see a person, neither a problem nor a burden. To be aware of human feelings, and respond to them directly.

I'll greet impersonality with character. I'll respond as a human being and expect to be treated thus

A job that draws you. You must be drawn, not driven. When you are, you forget about lunch.

MILLICENT FENWICK

The right job, the kind of work that fits us, is a true blessing. Whatever we do, if we forget about lunch or don't want to leave at five o'clock, the job is right.

Work is a basic part of our lives. It can define who we are. As much quality time is spent at work as at home. Our work relationships can be basic ones in our lives. Work generally takes a good eight or more hours out of our twenty-four.

To be drawn to a job instead of driven by it is a good sign. It's great when work is a challenge, stimulating, exciting; a boss is a friend who understands and can communicate; an office is a creative place to be instead of a prison. We like being with other people at work. Work is not separate from life, but an integral part of it. Work is fun as well as effort, something to be looked forward to. It is an essential part of ourselves.

I'll find meaning in my work.

I am divorced, poor, out of work and insurance, and my dreams are crushed by bankers. At fifty-seven, it is hard to keep dreaming.

But you must. Without your dreams, what have you got?

We must never let ourselves become trapped within a negative vision of life. We are not meant to be victims. *Victim* is a bad word. We can reject it, with all its connotations of helplessness and despair.

Possibility is always ahead of us as long as we are breathing. Victimization is a self-perpetuating exercise in futility. It is a vicious cycle and leads nowhere except to more of the same. Some of us feel at times: "I am a throwaway." "My dreams are crushed." "I am out of everything I need." These require responses. Only we can make the responses: "I am not a throwaway." "My dreams cannot be crushed." "It's time to let the past be the past, and I will find new needs." Our dreams need to be understood as parts of The Dream. It is about liberation and fulfillment. The Dream tells us unequivocally that we can start over.

My life starts today. I'm starting to dream.

MARCH 20

For when you offer yourself in service, it opens your own heart so that you may once again taste the sweetness of your own heart's innate compassion.

RAM DASS

We are basically good. We want the best for ourselves and everybody else. Thorns grow in our garden when we succumb to envy, hatred, meanness of spirit, smallness of purpose, and occasionally even trod over our ideals in the dirt.

The innate compassion of our heart, however, is a wise and loving guide. It calls us back to what is best for us—and is also the best part of us. It reminds us that we live in a world with other people. It reminds us sharply that there can be no peace or sweetness for us if we refuse to share these with others.

To offer ourselves in service is to open our heart. It means turning our back on aloneness, isolation, enthralled self-interest, and not giving a damn. It trains us to look out for the needs of others. It trains our conscience to be caring. It trains our nature to be nurturing. It calls us to become our best.

Today, I'll look outside myself. Where am I needed? I'll offer my help to another.

MARCH 21

Don't ever tell this gal that peace does not exist! I found strength in peace after battling alcoholism for years, and weakness most of my life.

Isn't peace wonderful? It isn't far away at all. It's here. We can share it.

Imprisonment within fear, hatred, or substance abuse is a killer. Many of us know it well. Daily battle with it is a hard story, with many ups and downs, defeats and victories. Always, the judgments and pains of others are involved, too.

Weakness is something we all share in one form or another. No one is strong without it. However, our weakness needs to be turned into strength. How can we do it? By working at it, refusing to give up, and seeking help when we need it instead of proudly trying to rely on our own resources. To get well requires support, networking, honesty, self-examination without flinching, and a vision of health and wholeness. Such a vision at our darkest hour can serve as the hinge of the door. The door is peace. We can walk through the door. It is open.

Peace may be close at hand, among my friends and ordinary surroundings. I'll claim it.

The necessity for patience had aged her magically; she was content in her age.

JOYCE CAROL OATES

Patience is one of the greatest of gifts. It can't be faked. It's real or it isn't. When it is, a person is gifted with a remarkable inner peace and contentment.

The necessity for patience doesn't always mean that patience wins out, however. Often we battle necessity with the zeal of a crusader. Ironically, we have manifold resources to work against our own self-interest and good, and we know how to use them. But when we're finally strong enough and wise enough to bow to necessity, great miracles can open up for us.

One of these is patience itself. It is an enormous help in aging when we confront the years that lie ahead. We look out upon the whole mystifying, wondrous, emerging vista of coming years. Patience enables us to take the next immediate step.

I'll aim for patience in my life. It may take time.

At seventy-seven I enjoy the typewriter my children gave me for my seventy-fifth birthday, write a poem now and then, correspond with old friends, play the piano at home and in two nursing homes, and enjoy my life to the best of my ability.

To enjoy life to the best of our ability is a secret of living at any age. The key words here are *enjoy* and *ability*. It takes a certain ability to enjoy. Far too many people, sadly, do not enjoy life much at all. When this occurs, something is seriously the matter. We're meant to enjoy life. Savor it. Appreciate it.

Our enjoyment of life needs to be based less on what we're supposed to enjoy than what we do enjoy. We can't follow an etiquette book here. Moral platitudes are out of place. It's just us, here, and reality, there—with nothing in between. If we've been behaving like robots all these years, pretending to enjoy what others thought we should, it's clearly time to find out the truth. Other people's opinions don't matter nearly as much as our own.

Where is the pleasure in my life? It's what keeps me alive. I'll make time for more.

MARCH 24

All I can do is to try not to isolate her; is to hold her when she is afraid; is to accept her as she is, a part of this family, without whom we would be less complete.

MADELEINE L'ENGLE

An elderly, sick person can feel brutally isolated. What does caring mean? To be held when one is afraid is something all of us want at any time of our life. This is an act of love.

Just as important is to be accepted as we are. Yet so often this is not granted to us. So often we do not grant this to other people, either. We refuse if they do not meet our expectations of correct behavior. We refuse if they are too troublesome or needy. We refuse if they get too much in our way.

This is a difficult, thorny, complex problem. Increasingly, it confronts children of older people. Crises abound. There are diseases that attack mind and body, crippling the human spirit, causing untold pain. There are few easy answers. However, there are guidelines. Try to avoid making a person feel, or be, isolated. Hold someone who is afraid; do not be afraid yourself. Most important, accept people as we are, not simply as others would have us be.

Whatever the fears and difficulties I encounter, today I'll offer unconditional love.

MARCH 25

Relaxation is the real answer to physical and emotional problems, I'm always told. Who can relax when the burdens of life are so heavy?

It's exactly when the burdens of life are so heavy that we need to relax. Sadly, we make relaxation appear to be yet another heavy burden, an unsolvable problem. It isn't.

To relax means letting go of the tension in our body. Slouch in a chair or lie on a bed. Let the shoulders drop. Breathe deeply and consciously—in and out, in and out. Sustain the breathing. Relax a finger, then a hand, then an arm. Relax a toe, then a foot, then a leg. Imagine floating.

To relax also means letting go of the tension in our mind. If there is an obsessive and heavy thought or problem, turn away from it for a moment. Focus elsewhere. See a fountain, an ocean, a lake, a valley. A dog, a cat, a horse, a fish. Bright yellow, burnt orange, turquoise, sea blue, red, white, black, mauve. A pine tree, a rose bush. A city street, a country road, a building, people walking, people running, people surfing. Think of something light or beautiful or uplifting.

I'll focus on hope and love. For a day, I'll relax.

In the night we were entertained by the sound of raindrops on the cedar splints which covered the roof, and awaked the next morning with a drop or two in our eyes.

HENRY DAVID THOREAU

Whenever we can, we need to get close to nature. Sometimes we can visit a great national park and view the rocks and trees, streams and waterfalls, and get close to them. If we are near an ocean or a lake, we can spend time on one of the greatest treasures remaining in the world—a beach.

Perhaps our way of drawing close to nature is to visit a nearby park. Savor the peace there. Watch and listen to a rising and falling fountain of water. Sit beneath a tree. Chat with a friendly bird. Feast our eyes on beautiful flowers. Walk on the grass.

We may have our own garden, large or small, where soil and plants need caring for. A tiny oasis in the midst of a fast-moving world. A place where a hummingbird pays a friendly call, a bee stops to buzz briefly, a pet dozes in the sun.

I'll turn my attention to nature. I'll allow myself to be touched by it.

I went into clinical depression. It was so severe I felt that I was in hell. Then, in my treatment, I met precious souls who did not require me to be perfect. They allowed me to be me.

What an extraordinary gift you have received. You are fortunate and blessed.

Why do we so often establish perfection as a guideline for other people and ourselves? Perfectionism is a curse. No one can ever attain it. First, we set up impossible standards to reach, then we berate others and ourselves when we automatically fail.

To strive to be perfect in a family, a marriage, or any relationship is to offer the kiss of death. No one can live or breathe naturally around perfectionism. It is unyielding. And it's terrible when someone who has "failed" to be perfect is expected to ask for forgiveness. One of the most precious gifts in the whole world is to allow other people to be themselves. A further step is to love them for themselves. This means accepting their absence of perfection.

I resolve to not be perfect.

Observing the people in repose, in the act of reflection, Father Latour was thinking how each of these people not only had a story, but seemed to have become his or her story.

WILLA CATHER

The idea is a fascinating one. It increases the value of our stories. It means that behind each story there lurks a flesh-and-blood person.

What I particularly like is that we can change our story. Our story is not finished until we are. Why do so many people completely overlook this? They become trapped, caught in the wiles of their own story, and make no effort at all to come up with a different ending than what is indicated by what has transpired before.

Our stories are incredible. So are we. We have the chance to write our own chapters, especially our own endings. Our stories are not histories so long as we're alive. They are stories in the process of being told, as over a campfire on a moonlit night. We are writing our own stories constantly as we live. We can introduce new characters and settings at will. Yes, we can even change ourselves radically, along with our stories. What an opportunity we have.

I have a hand in my story. Today, I'll think about the next chapter.

I have a terminal disease and live one day at a time. I dwell on a hill, and my vegetable and flower garden is at the bottom. I get my exercise going up and down the steps.

All of us must live one day at a time. But most of us don't realize it. We foolishly assume we have forever. We waste time, energy, and love.

We are all going to die. Death appears to be the only true form of democracy. Whether we arrived on the *Mayflower* or a slave ship, none of us is leaving by first class.

Meanwhile, life beckons us. A day at a time, a step at a time, is the only plan that is really open to us. Why do we become so impatient with this? We want to leap up to reach the top of Mt. Everest without ever having learned to climb. We want to become opera stars without taking singing lessons. We hope to win a lottery, yet refuse to start a small savings account. Our worst mistake is to place our wished-for destination in life in front of us as if it were a carrot, blot out everything else, and miss the joys of the trip.

I'll respond to life today, and savor it. I won't look ahead with trepidation.

MARCH 30

I train myself for triumph by knowing it is mine, no matter what.

AUDRE LORDE

Our attitude is terribly important. Do we feel we're doomed to lose? If so, the odds are we will. Or, do we believe with all our heart that triumph is meant for us?

The key is to concentrate on the task at hand. Remember, it is not a moment to assess our possibilities, to carefully weigh our merits and demerits, to daydream about the glamour of success. All our concentration must be centered upon the next step we need to take. Then, we must simply take it.

A great example of this is found in the game of tennis. A player cannot win and at the same time concentrate on his or her opponent and all the psychological and emotional luggage that accompanies such a look. Nor can a player spend time remembering the last game lost, and why. The immediate next step is to get the ball over the net successfully. That's all. Concentration is essential because this moment may make all the difference. A necessary companion of concentration is confidence. Triumph belongs to us. We must know it.

I'll bring concentration to what I do, and bolster it with confidence.

MARCH 31

Forty flower bulbs were planted in my backyard. This requires three walks a day out there to see if they have surfaced. I hope you can perceive what simple, crazy little things I find meaning in.

The best meaning is often found in little, simple things that can be described as very ordinary, and tend to be overlooked.

Think of the deep meaning in a family meal. Food that was grown and transported to a market has now found its way to preparation in a kitchen, and thence to a family meal. The hot bread, the roast, the vegetables and salad, and the wine await the common joy of their consumption.

Simple, crazy little things throughout our lives are the true sacraments that mark our human passage. Pretentious, big things are granted too much honor in our society. We hear about the big movie or building, corporation or church, book or salary. Meaning is frequently obliterated by bigness, which gets in the way and attracts all the attention. We need to look patiently between the cracks of life to find what rests there as a gift.

My life is full of meaning. Today, I'll find it in the unexpected places.

APRIL 1

They have no right to get old. I envy people whose parents died when they were young, that's easier to remember, they stay unchanged.

MARGARET ATWOOD

Change is the one constant factor in our lives. When we resist it or come to hate it, we limit ourselves and our capacity to live successfully.

Change just happens. Our relationships change because the people in them—including ourselves—are in flux. There is no way to bottle a moment's happiness and keep it forever. Our jobs change, too, because our work situation is always moving from here to there, with new elements injecting themselves. Our parents change. So do children.

There is no use saying we're tired of it and wish it would go away. It won't. We inflict pain on loved ones when we wish them to remain "as they were," instead of encouraging them to grow and mature and change. They need our help to keep growing, take on new dimensions of spirit and soul. The need is reciprocal. To grow in wisdom and become rich with years is our right.

Today, I stop running from an old enemy. I'll welcome change.

As I grow older, younger people help me stay in touch with new ideas by occasionally shocking the hell out of me.

There is always something that's even newer than what's new. We live on the edge of continuing discoveries, revelations, and creations.

What's new does not always come from someone who is young. But the adage that the young see visions while the old dream dreams holds a lot of truth. Older people had an earlier chance to see visions, wrestle with their meanings, and contribute ideas that probably shocked their elders at the time.

When a newer generation appears, inevitably there are new styles, expressions of personal identity, causes of social justice, and forms of behavior. Some of these have past counterparts, others do not. Shock value can be extremely helpful when it enables us to focus on a problem in an altogether different way, and see alternatives and possibilities we could not even imagine before.

I resolve to be open to what's new and different, even when it "shocks" me.

Baseball skill relates inversely to age. The older a man gets, the better a ball player he was when young, according to the watery eye of memory.

ROGER KAHN

Self-esteem is an essential ingredient of life. It is a gift when we have a good feeling about ourselves.

Some of us nurture self-worth, creating good humor around it. We all enjoy the scene when someone makes us laugh, providing us with a bounce of optimism and a needed injection of hope. That person shows the world a face that is determinedly buoyant.

At other times, however, we all experience moments when we can't seem to play such a helpful role. Life's burdens become too heavy for us to carry happily. Or our memories momentarily fail us, make us feel sad, and decrease our sense of self-worth. We can turn this around. If we weren't the best when we were young, there's nothing to prevent our being the best now. This is the present. Live in it!

I'll allow the full possibility of the present moment to buoy me up.

APRIL 4

Two of the most important words in the world are *thank you*.

Insecurity, shyness, and pride often stand in our way when we want to say *thank you*. When we learn how, though, we can build bridges between people.

Expressing thanks is not at all a Pollyanna-ish or sentimental thing to do. It requires grit, earnestness, and hard work, and can be complicated. For example, it isn't always easy for us to accept thanks. This is because we are acutely aware of our shortcomings and often feel unworthy of being thanked.

We need to say *thank you* to others more often than we do. To a stranger who helps us and whom we will probably never see again. To a co-worker who manages a smile of greeting every day for ten years, listens to our problems, and offers support. To a friend who is present in a moment of our great need, and comforts us. To a teacher who patiently works with us, finding promise hidden deep within us, and makes us see it, too. To someone close to us who loves us, and whom we have simply taken for granted.

I have much to be grateful for. Where there's someone to thank, I'll voice my gratitude. I won't leave something so important unsaid.

As long as we leave care of the soul out of our daily lives we will suffer the loneliness of living in a dead, cold, unrelated world.

THOMAS MOORE

Body, mind, and soul: These make up who we are. Why do some people try to emphasize one and downgrade the others? This can lead to a serious imbalance.

Care of the body is perhaps the simplest. At least, we spend more time on it. We diet, attempt to consume less fat and cholesterol, exercise to keep fit, and visit a doctor and a dentist regularly. However, none of these is enough unless we care very deeply about our body and its well-being.

Care of the mind? It is a lifelong task. From our earliest experience of schooling, this requires vivid imagination and tireless effort. Books and music, art and theater, inform our intellect and conscience.

The soul? It lies at the very heart of our being. It animates our life. It relates our body and mind to the rest of the world and wholeness of life. Care of the soul requires the same kind of daily nurturing that we willingly provide for a beautiful garden that we love.

Today I resolve to consider my soul and its needs—then set about providing for it.

We need to learn how not to cry over spilled milk.

What's done is done. We can't recall angry words we just uttered, and clearly regret. We can't erase the past five years from our consciousness.

Granted. Yet it's futile to play a bad scene over and over again in our mind. To wallow in anguish. To feel a martyr or a villain in dozens of reruns of a life scene. Doing it drains our energy. It can inflict permanent damage on our close relationships.

The best thing to do with spilled milk is get a rag or sponge and clean it up. Quickly. But to say it isn't there is both silly and impossible. It is there. Having cleaned it up, our next task is to see what effects the spill had. Did it have any effect on us? On other people? Was there a reason the milk got spilled? What was it? Let's try to understand what happened. Talk about it. What's done is done, but, like a pebble in a lake, it can cause ripples for a long time to come.

Today, I'll resolve an old conflict. My reward will be the relief of a clean slate.

APRIL 7

I was talking, as usual, mostly to hear
myself talk.

LARRY MCMURTRY

Why do we make communication so formidable a task?
It should be fairly simple: Someone talks, someone else
listens, they reverse roles, and soon they understand
what is on the mind of the other.

Easy? Often it doesn't work out that way. Frequently
we don't say what we mean; we cover up the truth. Is it
our intention to tell the truth in small doses? But doing
this can sometimes mean telling a lie. To complicate
matters even more, the other person in our communication drama may be doing exactly the same thing we are.
This means, at the very least, that there's lots of static on
the line. Under these circumstances, speaking and listening do not result in understanding.

Add body language. What our body says may contra-
dict what our words say. Our words signify peace, but
our attitude is warlike.

Finally, talking itself may get in the way. To listen is
far more important in communication than to speak.

I'll keep communication simple today: I'll listen.

My ritual of sameness, day after day, makes me feel simply numb. Can I change?

It's so easy for us to get locked inside a routine that seems to take over our life. Why do we let it?

There are innumerable ways to vary an existing routine, but they require our imagination and effort. All sorts of routines mark the maps of our daily lives. Going to work, going shopping, washing dishes, washing clothes, preparing meals, eating meals, watching TV, paying bills, putting out the garbage. On and on.

Driving to work, it's possible to discover an interesting new route. This lets us look at different streets, trees, buildings, billboards, and whatever comes into view. This is a small thing, but life is made up of small things. Or, take lunch. We don't have to go with the same people to the same place and have the same conversation. We can go for a walk. Locate a quiet spot and read. Eat an apple. You see? It's up to us. When we change small things, big things follow.

I'll try something totally out of character today. I'll dabble with change, and await the results.

The idea that one recovers from being in love is, of course, by definition (by my definition anyway) excluded from the state of love.

IRIS MURDOCH

The oddest thing about love is when it turns into hate. It can happen with a sense of betrayal, misunderstanding, or sometimes (it seems) a change in the weather from a trickle to a hurricane.

Hate, in all its complexity and intensity, is a distorted image of love. Indifference is what comes much closer to what we usually think of as hate. When we actually care enough to hate with deep passion, we somehow look into the mirror of love.

Do we ever cease to love when we have once loved? A million divorces would seem to say Yes. I wonder. If one looks closely, being in love and loving are not necessarily the same. Being in love can feel like intoxication or a high. Loving itself is quieter, maturer, more studied. It is a commitment of our whole personality.

Love has turned my life on its head before. I'm ready for it to happen again.

I often use the word *phony* to describe someone whom I dislike or oppose. Maybe I need to bring *phony* closer to home.

Some people set us off as if we were a firecracker. We dislike them instantly. Nothing they say or do is likely to meet with our acceptance. Of course, we're capable of setting off the same reaction in other people, too.

Phony is one of the most convenient epithets around. Like a large blanket, it covers a lot of territory. When we completely disagree with a politician, detest the work of a particular artist, or are out to get a neighbor, phony is perhaps the most effective charge to hurl. It's a bit like crying "Fire" in a crowded theater. It evokes attention, sounds an alarm.

However, how do we feel when someone accuses us of being phony? It's a tough charge to answer with clarity because, by virtue of its ambiguity, it is virtually unanswerable. It's buckshot. It's meant to clobber a person, to strike violently, batter and defeat. Let's banish *phony* from our vocabulary, try to understand, and say what we mean.

I'll take others as they are.

APRIL 11

I remembered that during the worst of my illness, when I had had some particularly great difficulty trying to learn to move that rigid left shoulder, or relax that always stubborn wrist, if I kept hammering at it, the next day would bring its reward in increased serenity and the beginning of learning.

MARGARET BOURKE-WHITE

Learning is inevitably a slow process. It has a gradual quality. Whenever we think we've learned all that is necessary, always there's more ahead.

The painstaking patience required by true learning is the teacher of serenity. We are required to give up our timetables and demands, agendas and plans. The bottom line is that we have to give up control, or at least our illusion of it. We don't have any! When we reach this moment of truth, surprising and wonderful things begin to happen to us. We may discover fresh reservoirs of strength deep within us. And, entirely new people and ideas, challenges and opportunities may flood into our life.

A secret is to remain flexible. There may come into our experience new solutions that make us laugh at their unpredictability.

Today I'll rely on patience to teach me serenity.

I'm older and more mature, but still I take myself too seriously.

It's a fine balance that we must sustain between not tak‑ing ourselves seriously enough and taking ourselves too seriously.

We deny ourselves essential dignity when we refuse to treat our life with respect and love. Our life is a wonder‑ful and incredible gift. To throw it on a dump heap of abuse or indifference is to deny its worth. We cannot let others denigrate our life, either. Our attitude of rever‑ence for all of life, including our own, is a means of sur‑vival.

We'll always wish to balance dignity with humor and humility. We are aware that life's a stage. Surely we know that our performance doesn't always deserve rave reviews. This makes us the same as other people. Let's share cen‑ter stage graciously with them. Applause and boos will be equally shared, too. Hopefully, we'll be able to smile at the whole show.

Do I take myself too seriously? Today, I'll aim for honesty and humility in presenting myself to others

If you follow your bliss, you put yourself on a kind of track that has been there all the while, waiting for you, and the life that you ought to be living is the one you are living.

JOSEPH CAMPBELL

How can we get our lives in shape? One way is to examine them carefully when they are all out of shape. What went wrong?

Maybe we did what we didn't want to do or like doing. Did we fail to use our skills well? Did we listen to the siren song of a false promise? Did we get tied up in a fantasy instead of roaming free in reality?

The good news? We can turn around. The right track is waiting for us to find it. We are not consigned to misery and failure. We can start living our life the way it's meant to be. However, more furious effort on our part to find the answer may not be the answer. Instead it might be time for quiet reflection, an inward look, discernment of truth. This begins with finding a quiet place and being quiet. We can make a resolution, too. A resolution to begin—gradually—a change toward the life we wish to live.

Today, I claim my life in all its glory

I am an eighty-year-old widower living with my "family" of five cats and a large dog.

Some people make a big mistake when they limit friends to the human race. Other friends, including animals, birds, and fish are available. Dogs and cats seem to be our most frequent companions.

While a dog wags its tail in devotion, a cat rotates a tail in anger. A dog licks our hand as a sign of affection, while a cat sits on our lap and scratches our knee. Both have healthy appetites. We must bathe our dog, whereas our cat attends personally to such an intimate matter. Each one knows instantly when it has done the right or wrong thing. One is salt, the other pepper.

Our dogs and cats are wonderful friends. A cat is easily put-out and impatient with us, mysterious and puzzling. It wakes us at dawn by getting up on our pillow and purring. A dog is quite patient, hardly ever selfish (except at mealtimes), and easy to live with (although surprisingly easily hurt). Dogs and cats are good family members.

I'm grateful for the family I have.

APRIL 15

Cremains! There are no ashes—they're ground-up bone fragments, if you want to know the truth. I saw my wife die, and whatever became of her next has got nothing to do with that stuff in the box on my mantel.

The passage from life to death remains, in nearly everyone's consciousness, the most important journey we ever take.

The passage of a loved one is as compelling to us as our own. We can agonize over this, spend sleepless nights, have troubled dreams. We ask the question: How can we find peace? This question stands out in stark relief. Whether a loved one's body has been buried deep in the earth, or its ashes scattered on the sea or kept in a container, our relationship to the departed is still very much alive.

Have we forgiven anything that might still stand between us that was unresolved? Have we accepted forgiveness for any anxiety or pain that we believe we may have inflicted upon the departed? Have we been able to let go—and let our beloved go freely? We need to grant our loved one Godspeed on his or her journey that now continues. And, finally, we need to accept his or her blessing upon our continuing life here.

The loved ones I've lost would wish me happiness, not grief. Today, I'll try to give them that.

APRIL 16

Caring for my elderly father often makes me very upset. Then he gets upset. Then my husband tells me I'm cruel to my father.

Intergenerational relations can be subtle and complex Often roles are reversed when, for example, a parent moves into the dependent position of a child, and a child suddenly realizes he or she has assumed parental responsibilities.

Caring for anyone is a tricky business. It involves our attitude as well as our work. In caring, do we feel that the person we are helping is vastly inferior to us, or manipulating us, or taking advantage of us? Does caring irritate us or stir up resentments? Is it, in our view, a waste of our time, an intrusion on our life, an exercise in futility? Does the person we are caring for seem ungrateful?

Feelings need to be sorted out. Do we really want to care for someone else? What are the ground rules? Is it possible to have amicable terms of mutual communication?

I'll credit myself for the care I give others. And I'll replenish that ability to care by caring for myself

Sometimes, for a brief span—while sweeping the basement, watching crows on the snow, playing backgammon with JH—I'll experience a surge of absolute happiness.

NED ROREM

The best moments of happiness are often surprises. They have little to do with profundity. But we must give ourselves permission to be surprised.

It's a shame when we block the flow of happiness and erect barriers to keep it out. Happiness is so simple a thing and defies conventional definitions. Money, power, prestige, and authority cannot guarantee happiness at all. It comes much closer to serendipity. Fortunate accidents are small miracles.

Brother Lawrence found spiritual meaning in cleaning kitchen pots and pans. We draw close to nature, hearing and seeing its marvelous ordinary miracles, when we listen to rain fall on a wooden roof, work quietly in a garden tending flowers and plants, or watch the wonder of an early morning sky illumined by a solar light. We need to be open to the epiphanies of life's surprises.

I'm going to let absolute happiness touch my life today. I won't keep it at bay.

Whether we're old or young, we're all together in a jet plane called life. We might as well try to enjoy the trip.

The mix of people in our common life is amazing. Someone is always being born while someone else is about to enter high school; yet others just got married, started a promising new job, retired from work, or are holding a new grandchild.

We're all in life together. Older people need to remember what it was like to be young. How it felt to fall in love for the first time. How much courage it took to go out on that initial job hunt. How painful was that awful sense of failure when the whole world seemed about to collapse.

Younger people need to see older ones as people, not statistics standing in their way or stereotypes that are objects of ridicule. Young women and men need to find role models of aging and mentors among their older friends—people whom they genuinely admire for their perseverance, and respect for their contributions to life. Human experience is incredibly similar, and neither youth nor age changes it essentially.

I won't let my the expectations of my age color my reactions to life. I'll respond from the core of my being.

My fiftieth birthday was quite unlike my fortieth, but equally memorable, and lots funnier. I always remind people about my birthdays; nobody is ever able to say, "But why didn't you tell me?"

MADELEINE L'ENGLE

Birthdays are punctuation marks in our lives. They break a pattern of sameness. They are invariably interesting and stand out.

Pride in birthdays is the healthiest way of dealing with them. But some people try to hide a birthday, feel shame or fear about aging, and refuse to greet a new year with a smile. However, I think most of us tend to love a birthday—any birthday—and find it festive and promising. It's like a party, a chance to share.

If nobody close to us is around at the moment of our birthday, we should seek an acquaintance or even a stranger who might be delighted to celebrate with us. We need to celebrate our birthday. There's something child-like and wondrous about the event. It remembers when someone was born. Us. Now there is celebration of birth, growth, and life.

I won't let anyone miss the good news of my birthday.

APRIL 20

I had to cope with being a widow and found helping others is my answer. If I have something to look forward to, and someone who needs me, I feel better.

When we're hurting and in need, our immediate salvation is to get outside ourselves. Grieving is natural and necessary, yet it is important to place it in perspective.

It is possible to become obsessed by grief. To look inward and to the past. To feel our energy sapped. To have no reason to get up in the morning. To want to retreat into an opium den–like ambiance, move into forgetfulness, embrace fantasy.

Life waits. Others need us. There is work to be done that only we can do. Our love is needed. Our sense of hope is required where otherwise there might be no hope. Our contribution is essential. We matter. We can make all the difference. We feel better when we have the courage to respond to a need, and look forward to it.

I'll allow someone else's need to fuel my journey.

Almost all people, whether they are potential or actual grandparents, have practiced certain forms of economy in their day, even if they are not like my own grandmother, who practiced it her whole life.

M. F. K FISHER

To practice some forms of economy is beneficial for virtually anyone. It helps to maintain a balance between excess, on the one hand, and deprivation, on the other. In addition, it allows us to appreciate what we have and treat it with respect.

In most of our lives there are times when we seem to have more than we need, other times when we seem to have less. Some of us remember living in the depression of the early 1930s. It had a *Titanic*-like quality. The catastrophe struck ruthlessly and unexpectedly; the bottom fell out without warning. Never again could we take anything for granted. Any image of security would forever after have a question mark dangling over it. Any safe haven would be suspect.

There is a fundamental lesson to be learned from the experience. In times when we possess what we call the good life, it is wise to store up provisions for a rainy day. An umbrella can't save us.

I'll aim for balance in my economy.

It seems to me we're already dead if we live only in our memories.

Memories are terribly seductive when they insatiably make love to our longings and caress our imaginations.

All of us have memories. It's natural and healthy to welcome and enjoy them. They become a problem, however, when they cause us to lose interest in our life right now. This is when we prefer the past. We move into it. Finally, we live in the past.

We can't, though. Trying to makes us become discombobulated to an alarming degree. We're neither fish nor fowl, here nor there. What a mess! If we add an addiction to this, we can find ourselves in serious trouble. The answer is an uncomplicated one. This is it: We need to get up, walk to the nearest window, open it, lean outside, feel a breeze on our face, give a hearty shout, and decide—right now in this very instant—to rejoin the human race.

Today, I resolve to look straight ahead, honoring my memories, but expecting to make new ones.

Ann was the sort of woman all men idealized if they noticed her, but very few men would have the courage or sense to want to marry her.

JANE RULE

I'm tired of people who take passing note of me, then construct a convenient image of their own choice, and claim to know me. Aren't you tired of this in your own life, too?

Some people like to idealize us; others denigrate us. Seldom do they draw close enough to see the wounds we bear, the joys we have to share. It can be frustrating, even maddening on occasion.

We are ourselves guilty of the same thing. We pass by too quickly, making a judgment without stopping to learn the truth. We create an image that denies another person's real humanity. We move on and avoid an honest relationship. At times we place someone on a pedestal we have built; at other times we subject a person to painful criticism and gossip, without pausing to know the flesh-and-blood reality. Let's change, and make an effort to know one another.

I'll look closer at one I thought I knew. I'll peer more diligently at a new face. I'll make the extra effort to *know* another.

APRIL 24

There's no way out.

Life is not constructed as a medieval fortress. It is a vast, intricate network, with infinite and subtle connections. It's important to remember that there's always a way in and a way out.

When we're confronted by seemingly insurmountable problems, it's easy to feel claustrophobic and shut in. The walls seem to be pressing ever closer. There is no window to see through. No doorway appears as a possible exit. It seems that we are a victim like the tragic figure in Edgar Allan Poe's *The Pit and the Pendulum*, who cannot escape a terrible fate, and even has to watch as it approaches.

This is precisely the moment when we need to visualize an alternative of liberation. We see beyond the threatening walls that seem ready to crush us. We see through the monstrous weight poised to destroy us. Now a way out appears. We see we're in a fluid situation, with lots of openings.

I'll open a window. I'll step through a doorway. I'll find an opening today.

After all, van Gogh was depressed and
Beethoven had a poor time of it. The prophet
Hosea, if you will recall, had a bad home life.

WALKER PERCY

Some of the great achievers of history had an intimate
knowledge of pain, infirmity, depression, and bad days.
Why should we be spared what they weren't?

At moments we seem to expect a perfect rose garden
in our lives. In fact, we want perfection on a silver platter
and a rose garden to boot. The root of this may be a wish
to have no problems. Everything should be wrapped in a
neat package (we say) and handed us as a gift, complete
with a red ribbon.

We're going to have to work for what we desire,
whether it's a fulfilling relationship or a fulfilling job, a
bank account or a dream vacation. More to the point,
we'll face obstacles both within and outside of ourselves.
It's how we face and deal with the obstacles that makes
the difference. Faced with their own problems, van Gogh
kept painting, Beethoven composing, Hosea doing his
work as a prophet. I guess it's up to us.

I won't let excuses keep me from doing what I
need to do.

APRIL 26

Say kind things—not lies, but true kind things.

Our tongue can be a formidable weapon. Gossip that starts on the wind can become a killer of a tornado.

Unkind things get too frequently uttered. It's somewhat akin to the fact that good news is not considered news. For example, a peaceful protest march of three hundred thousand people may rate four paragraphs in a small news story on page thirty of a metropolitan newspaper; yet a stabbing that takes place during the march will probably move the story to page one.

If we want to get someone else's attention, it's sad that a violent, shocking, and yes, unkind story is more apt to succeed than a tender and kind one. A firecracker is more effective than a hand on a shoulder in arousing an immediate response. Maybe we should surrender the idea of an immediate response, be more patient, and try nonviolent ways to gain attention. We could start to create a more peaceful world.

I'll wait before I speak, weigh the circumstances, and let a more peaceful world begin with me

APRIL 27

The young man who has not wept is a savage, and the old man who will not laugh is a fool.

GEORGE SANTAYANA

Half-laughing, half-crying may be the best combination. How can anyone not cry and laugh? It seems to me life requires both. There is tragedy and joy, sadness and happiness, and our response should always be an honest one.

Some men and women of any age strive to be stoical and never weep, even in the face of great misfortune and loss. Others feel it is frivolous and reveals a lack of seriousness if we laugh. Yet laughing and crying are very close. They open up human emotion. They elicit a response from others. They manifest a genuine sense of what is poignant and deeply felt.

We should feel sorry for someone who cannot cry. He or she apparently lacks the freedom to express strong feelings. But someone who refuses to laugh under any circumstances is, it seems to me, a fool. My advice is to wise up and have a belly laugh.

I'll feel free to cry and laugh when it's honest.

APRIL 28

I want to commune quietly with life instead of using it as a racetrack.

It's up to each of us, to a great extent, how we choose to treat life. We can be gentle or fierce, hating or loving, cold or warm, accepting or rejecting. We can also work out our own combinations of these.

A combination may be our wisest choice. For example, we may not have enough control over the elements in our life to be able either to commune quietly alone or to move quickly in the fast race. Instead, a smattering of each might be necessary for us. We can learn how to meditate quietly at certain moments and, at the same time, be involved in the action of life.

Living is an art. It requires sensitivity as well as commitment, tender awareness along with strong zeal. Most of us cannot go off by ourselves to live in a quiet outpost of the global village. However, we can often both define and determine the quality of life that we want.

Today, I'll find a point of quiet and stay there for a while.

APRIL 29

Oh, I feel terrible. Rotten, I feel. I've got Spring Misery.

DOROTHY PARKER

Spring can conjure up all sorts of mixed reactions. The poet T. S. Eliot went so far as to call April the cruelest month.

Whenever the seasons turn, I guess our emotions become involved. The first sign of spring sharply reminds us that the long, frozen winter will end soon. Spring itself brings green verdure, fresh buds, a stirring of long dormant feelings, a promise of release.

This requires an adjustment. Spring blues are different from winter blues. In the spring there's a kind of exuberance and a hint of deliverance. When new hope appears, we still have to deal with past guilt, failure, and grieving. So, it's necessary to give ourselves permission to live again and risk again. It helps when days are balmier, nature is awakening, and we can balance the past with the inevitability of coming change.

Today, I'll let myself appreciate spring for what it's worth, without fear or sadness.

Can I learn how to grow old? If so, who can teach me?

We have to be able to live as fully as possible at each stage of our life. When we're growing up, peers are our best teachers. We learn from each other.

Growing older, role models become increasingly important. We observe people who have managed to age with charm, care, and wisdom, and other people admire and love them.

Finally, it comes down to ourselves. We must learn how to grow old and need to teach ourselves. Why not? We've had a lifetime to learn. We know a lot more than when we started out. We've been burned on occasion, felt the sting of adversity and the whip of cruelty, sunk into the morass of failure. Not only do we know about life, but also about ourselves—the games we play, our strengths and weaknesses, the ruses we are adept at, and the sense of meaning that can be found at the deepest part of us. We can become our own best teachers about how to grow old.

I resolve to learn one new thing every day.

Man is always a spectator. . . . We're spectators of our own lives. I've done it since I was born.

GRETA GARBO

The best show in town is people. We observe the conduct and actions of others constantly, especially movie and sports stars, bona fide royalty, and politicians.

We keep track of our own lives best. There is more than a bit of narcissism in all of us. We catch quick glances of ourselves in mirrors at unsuspecting moments, gaze at full-length images of ourselves in reflecting shop windows while we walk on the street.

What do we think when we see ourselves so candidly? The truth is that we have already created our own public images for others to see. So our image may reflect strong extroversion even if we're shy, sophistication even if we're untutored and simple, generosity even if we have a natural Scrooge-like nature. We do put our best foot forward. This is all right if we maintain a sense of humor about it, know what we're doing, and never lose contact with who we really are.

Today, I'll explore who I really am instead of who I'm supposed to be.

MAY 2

They once said not to trust anybody over thirty or forty. What has age to do with trust? Wouldn't someone older be more trustworthy?

Deciding whom we may trust is a tricky business. We are looking for people who have ideals, a sense of inherent goodness, a strong honest streak, and a touch of unselfishness.

Young or old may fill the bill. It isn't a question of age. It concerns individual commitment. There is a view, however, that corruption grows with age; so do selfishness and cynical adaptation to the status quo. Nonsense! Balderdash!

There are hucksters, egomaniacs, manipulators, exploiters, and sellouts both young and old. We find as many older men and women who fight for justice as young ones; as many young men and women who struggle for needed social change as old ones. The big question is: How trustworthy do we manage to be?

Whom do I trust in my life? What is it about them that inspires belief? I'm going to look for those qualities, and cultivate them in my own life.

MAY 3

I have acquaintances but no friends. I used to hope that one day a friend would appear. Now, a senior citizen for years, I have lost that hope.

Who is a friend? It takes one to know one. The best way to have friends is to be a friend. It's not a terribly complicated affair. We can try reaching out to others instead of waiting for them to reach out to us.

In other words, initiate the act of giving. Does this make us vulnerable? Yes. Is it a risk? Definitely. Yet without vulnerability and risk, life isn't worth living. How good a friend are we? Are we patient, loyal, open to changes, resistant to gossip, nonjudgmental, ever present in times of someone else's need?

Perhaps we drive away potential friends by our own self-preoccupation, seeming indifference, coldness, and apparent lack of interest in their feelings. If a new friend appears in the distance, and comes closer, try to greet this unique person with warmth and caring. The best thing to do? Appear as a new friend to someone else.

Friendship is a sacred gift. I'll honor it.

I'm not doing what I want to do with the precious time I have left.

In certain moments of unusual clarity we are able to see ourselves, and our lives, in a sudden shock of recognition.

We can see what is good and what is lacking. When we're conscious of the shortness of remaining time, it's possible for us to make significant decisions. For example, if something makes us unhappy, we can change it or remove it from our life. If something else represents an agony or a failure for us, we can refuse to let it block our view of wholeness.

The precious time we have left assumes major importance. In terms of decision making, it is a question of now or never. The actress Gloria Swanson wisely noted that never is a long, undependable time, and life is too full of rich possibilities to have restrictions placed on it. *Now* is a much more positive and energizing word than *never*, which is negative, imprisoning, stultifying, and reproaches our possibilities. We need to decide now to do what we want with the time we have.

I'm going to cut the word *never* out of my vocabulary, and make *now* the thrust of my life.

My seventy-two-year-old mother eats better than I do, practices yoga, and goes to two aerobics classes a week. But she completely resigned herself to never having sex again after she and my father divorced ten years ago. She tried dating, but it's really hard for an educated older woman to meet interesting men who aren't scared off.

We can't, despite our best intentions, prescribe what is best for someone else. We mistakenly try to project our own ideas and feelings onto another person whom we love, yet really don't know as well as we think we do.

Anyone's sex life, or seeming lack of it, is a highly individual matter. Some people don't have sex, but channel their sexual energy knowingly and creatively into areas of work, friendship, recreation, and volunteerism.

Separating sex and love is difficult for a number of people who don't want one without the other. And there are women and men who loved deeply once, but feel unable or unwilling to enter into love again. We need to respect people's individual differences when it comes to sex and love, and support them in any way we can.

I'll try to give acceptance and support even when I don't fully understand another person.

Different parts of me are charging off in various directions today. I want unity of purpose in my life.

Each of us has a number of different people under our skin, trying to get ahead, occupy center stage, work and play.

It's up to us to relate kindly to the cast of characters under our skin. There are radicals and conservatives, romantic figures and very sober ones, lazy, laid-back funsters and hard-driving, ambitious go-getters. It requires all our wisdom, perseverance, and loving to relate to this mix of people. We don't like certain parts of ourself as much as others. Some even embarrass us and we try to disown them. This inevitably backfires because all these parts constitute us. They're who we are.

If we want unity of purpose in our life, we have to grant the different people under our skin equal time. Attempt to meet their demands, but make them realize they can't be relentlessly selfish. They need to realize that they are parts of our wholeness.

I resolve to make getting along with myself a full-time job.

I woke in tears this morning. I wonder whether it is possible at nearly sixty to change radically.

MAY SARTON

I think it's probably easier to change radically at sixty than at thirty. Why? Because as we grow older, we hoard experience. It is a great teacher.

Knowledge helps us make changes because we find out what works and what doesn't. After we've tried this route and that path, we should have a pretty good perspective on our journey's direction. We learn whom to trust, and why. When we discover history and herstory, we're not condemned to repeating it.

Knowledge opens up awareness, which leads to conviction. When there's not so much time left, we recognize how precious it is. There's no time to waste! If we've been carrying excess luggage in our life, we can dispense with it. If we've been repressing a great dream that incarnates our hope, we can honor the dream. This leads to the most radical change.

I am a vast repository of experience. I'll draw on it to make the most of the rest of my life.

My pain, my suffering, is burning me. I wish the strange fire might be still.

Pain is our universal human experience. None of us escapes it. Pain occurs in our body, in our mind, in our soul.

Trying to fight against pain is futile. It absorbs all our needed energy. Instead, we have to come to grips with it. Accept it. Let it in. Breathe with it. Move with it. Come to some kind of a truce with it. Get familiar with it. Even, on occasion, make friends with it.

Yes, we'll do everything we can to understand and treat pain's cause. There are many things we can do to alleviate it. Still, pain persists. It is a companion that stays unnaturally close to us. Once we have quit treating pain as a mortal enemy and have moved into a flexible relationship with it, we can begin to focus on something else. At that moment, pain can cease to be the center of our universe.

Today I'll recognize the pain, accept it, and go on to something else.

A happy childhood can't be cured.

HORTENSE CALISHER

Some people are blessed with near-perfect families, idyllic childhoods, and the best start possible in life.

Others, not so blessed, still end up very well. Having had to deal with adversity at an early age, they were forced to fend for themselves in order to survive and learned how to adapt in order to thrive amid life's vicissitudes.

Whether or not ours was a happy childhood, that particular phase of our life is long gone. How are we doing now? It's silly to linger surreptitiously over our departed childhoods. Yet some of us can't seem to get out. Our entire focus on life, including our relationships and work, is somehow stuck in childhood memory. On the one hand, if we had a happy childhood, we want to go back to it. On the other hand, if our childhood was unhappy, we may make the mistake of lingering, too: unable to forgive, embrace happiness, or move forward. The time has come to let childhood go.

I won't be locked inside any past moment. When it's necessary, I'll let the past go.

Like all aged men and women, he had his good days and bad days. Irreversibly now, he looked his age: a white halo of hair framed the deathly pallor of his face. Only the coal-dark eyes blazed undimmed.

BENITA EISLER

Good and bad days seem to follow all of us like shadows on a wall.

Our good days are usually described in terms of our being in top form, optimistic, healthy, productive, friendly, generous, sexy, creative, amusing, and likable. Our bad days frame us in poor form, pessimistic, sickly, unproductive, irritable, stingy, asexual, sloppy, sad, and grim.

We all prefer the good days, of course, in everybody else as well as ourself. It's hard to fake a good day when we're having a bad one. But it's clever to avoid extreme good *or* bad days, and find a space in the middle that is honest, congenial, workable, and amenable to others.

I'll look for a middle ground.

The sheer gratitude after coming through fire is so profound, so first-things-first, it makes you laugh inside when people say you are brave.

PAUL MONETTE

We are tested. Our life's journey has perils and rapids, loneliness and terror, physical pain and spiritual dilemmas.

Confronted by such things, we come to know the meaning of coming through fire. Usually we have little or no choice about when this occurs. Something happens to us. An accident breaks the easy continuity of our life, a job is suddenly gone, love grotesquely takes on a mask of hatred, betrayal leaps out at us from the shadows, peace becomes war—and we've got to deal with it.

These are times when, at whatever age we are, we grow up. They are part of the warp and woof of living. There is no escape from them. When we accept them, and work with them in creative ways, we grow by leaps and bounds. Our life takes on character and depth.

I'll welcome what tests me. I am ready to be made stronger.

I am retired, make do with a small pension and social security, and am writing a novel, making quilts, sewing, knitting, reading, listening to music, going places, and my life is great.

One of the greatest blessings is finding what we like to do, and doing it. There is nothing worse than doing day by day what we detest and find utterly boring and meaningless.

This holds true in all our lives, whether we're poor or rich, rural or urban, retired or in the workplace. It's really up to us, as individuals, to choose what sense we can make out of life. Opportunity is wide open. Someone holding down an eight-hour job can manage to have hobbies or volunteer in a neighborhood activity, pursue a personal goal or continue an education.

After retirement, it's entirely possible to open up a whole new world of creativity, challenge, and interest. In this case, "retirement" becomes something of a misnomer. A wealth of potential awaits us when we decide to seek new adventure, fresh goals, and maybe even an undiscovered continent we never dreamed of.

What is it that I really want to do? Why am I not doing it? Today, I'm going to set a goal and start toward it.

In those days you met anybody anywhere.

GERTRUDE STEIN

Does the past seem a better time? Friendlier, less violent, easier to cope with?

It was an age of manners and prescribed behavior. There was a studied public civility. Although there was as much violence, it was deliberately unseen. It's arguable that everybody knows more about everybody else today because telecommunications have made the world a global village. It's harder to hide famine or infidelity, political motives or public scandal. Of course, the pace of living was slower then. No cars or TV, no airplanes or fax machines.

Given present reality, how are we to live peacefully and well amid the constant flux of rapid change? There is no single, easy answer. But when we're confronted with a scene of enormous complexity, we can decide to unravel one small bit of it, period. Then another. Our pace is up to us.

This is my time. I claim it. I will handle it in my own way.

MAY 14

Cling onto any shred of better things to come. The best I can offer to anybody having difficulties is not to give up on hope.

There are isolated moments in our human life that seem to resemble hell. The bottom drops out. We are transfixed by pain, left stark naked by failure, embarrassed beyond our capacity to take it.

At such a moment we feel powerless. There seems little or nothing to hold onto. We have been stripped of pride. Nothing makes sense. This is precisely when we need to know there is something to hold onto, something to make sense. And there is. We've just got to find it or let it find us. This is a moment when our life can be saved. Wiser than before, we can go on living. We can pick up the pieces and start over.

Hope is our way to survive. It is the lifeline. A remarkable thing about hope is that we can bear it to each other. We are able to carry the lifeline to someone else, or receive it in a moment when it saves us.

When I'm sinking, I'll look for a lifeline. I'll find it when I need it.

For my father's funeral I had nothing to wear
and this posed a nagging problem all day long.
It was one of those problems, simple, or
impossible of solution, to which the mind
insanely clings in order to avoid the mind's
real trouble.

JAMES BALDWIN

Most of us are experts at using our minds for diversion-
ary purposes. We look away. Or, unable to deal with a
problem, we move on to something else.

While this can offer momentary release from a nagging dilemma, it solves nothing. The real problem is still
in our craw, waiting to baffle or haunt us. Expending our
time and energy on a mere diversion from what's bug-
ging us, we become more vulnerable than we know.

Now the problem is that when the real crisis strikes so
forcefully that we can't avoid it any longer, we've used up
our energy on something else and no longer have the resources to defend ourselves or make a clear judgment.
What can we do? Trust to luck. But it's best by far, the
next time we move into such a situation, to say a loud
No to any diversion and shore up our energy to confront
the basic, raw, real problem that will not go away until
we deal with it correctly.

I'll meet my problems head-on.

Growing older, a lot of people develop such peculiarities that they're hard to deal with and their personalities are intolerable.

I like to visit an aquarium and see all the different fishes there. They're dazzling in their diversity. They range all the way from a sea horse to a piranha, and in every imaginable color.

Watching human beings reminds me of visiting the aquarium. We are absolutely incredible. We are thin and fat, tall and short, old and young, in various hues of color, and all our personalities represent an unimaginable spectrum of diversity.

It's funny, but one person's idea of normalcy or acceptability is another person's idea of peculiarity. There is simply no norm recognized by everyone. Just look at us. We speak different languages, have different accents, like to eat different foods, come from different places, have different goals, cultivate different tastes, laugh at different things, worship in different ways, and even wear different clothing. Differences aside, we're all human. We need to get along and appreciate one another.

My peculiarities are part of what defines me. They're knots and bumps of experience. I appreciate them in myself, and in others.

What possesses us to hold onto these cream-colored papers our children scrawl on? I go through sheet after sheet that she attacked with crayons when she was only in nursery school.

FRANK DEFORD

Our memories can be very tangible. They are not only somewhere in our mind, but here, here in a photo album, a scrapbook, a pile of old letters and papers.

This is a precious gift. We can literally hold onto it. A photo album recreates past moments of great joy: A trip taken together, a family reunion, an anniversary, an evening with friends, a peaceful fragment of time on a Sunday afternoon.

We come across an old cardboard box in an attic. To our surprise it contains grandmother's recipe for jelly roll: 3 eggs, 1/2 cup sugar, 2/3 cup flour, 3/4 tsp. baking powder, butter a shallow pan, bake in a quick oven. Near the recipe is dad's last letter before he died, his writing wobbly.

I won't throw out my past. When the time is right, I'll drag out the trunk, take down the album, and reacquaint myself.

I'm recovering from a stroke and had to learn how to walk, dress, and do everything for myself again. A fresh focus helped.

We are frequently reborn in this life. When do we experience it? In coming back to health after an illness, recovering from addiction, moving to a new location, beginning a new relationship, or undertaking a wholly new venture.

It is remarkable that we can build a new life. It takes courage, discipline, and patience. A fresh focus is essential. It is as if we were to walk through a door, down a corridor, find a new door, discover it's not locked, open it, and walk through it into a fresh experience. Often it is an experience that is without precedent for us.

We can do this. We have enormous potential and virtually unlimited power to effect extraordinary change in our life when circumstances demand it or we will it. It's possible for us to return to square one, start over, and succeed.

There's no such thing as "too late." I'm willing to start over.

We must pray not just for the poor and
unfortunate, but with them.

JOHANN B. METZ

Detachment is important sometimes, but not when it
neutralizes or wipes out our sense of compassion.

The idea of *us* and *them* is not a good one. It isolates.
It stands in the way of empathy and working together.
Our sisters and brothers in the world don't want keepers;
they want sisters and brothers who care. So do we.

When we seek to help someone by acting for them—
but not with them—we assert our superiority and detachment. Often we feel we should be thanked for going
out of our way to do a good work. But what if it is
clearly our responsibility, even our duty? What if the ta-
bles were turned, and we needed help from others who
were in a position to provide it? Instead of being selfish
in hoarding what we possess, it is best for us to share in a
loving, understanding way.

I'll try seeing others as *you and me* instead of *us and
them.*

It is vital for us not so much to expect a miracle each day, but to accept the miracles as they are brought to us.

Our daily expectations need to be brought into balance with what life gives us. We can be decidedly unhappy if we have deep wishes out of sync with our possibilities and skills.

Let's try to make peace with life. Every day represents a miracle that we're here. A number of smaller miracles also come our way. These include acts of kindness, love, friendship, sustenance, and new possibilities that surprise us.

What can we do with the miracles? I suppose we can just take them for granted, dismiss them from our conscious thought, and treat them as if they were mundane and unneeded interlopers. Of course, an alternative is to feel gratitude for them as wonderful gifts that embolden and magnify our lives. Acceptance implies our openness to the miracle, when our empty hands are outstretched and filled.

Today I make peace with life. I'll be realistic about my wishes and demands. I'll welcome any miracles.

I had everything but love.

DIANA BARRYMORE

Having everything but love is a bit like being in the position of owning a gold mine that hasn't any gold.

A songwriter asked the question: What is this thing called love? Love is hard to put our finger on, yet it is everywhere. Love cannot be purchased, it is priceless. The secret of love is that it must be given in order to be received. We have to know how to receive it in order to give it. This eludes lots of people who don't know how to receive or wish to give.

When we feel love has escaped us, many of us react in a desperate kind of frustration because we're both hurt and angry. We can let sheer speed take over our lives and race our bodies as if they were track horses. We need to remember about love that it is patient and kind; not jealous or boastful; it does not insist on its own way. Love bears all things, believes all things, hopes all things, endures all things. That is St. Paul's definition.

I'm going to seek out the love around me. I'll strive to let love reign within me.

Envy is like a snake. It bit me. I need to get rid of the poison.

Envy is horrible. It transforms us from someone we know into a stranger. It can change us into a monster.

It's so unpredictable. Someone else receives honor, love, reward, and we go bonkers. Why? Envy is irrational. Suddenly we're confronted with someone else's well-being, and we can't stand it.

What is it that we want? What raises the shadow world into such a glaring distraction for us? Do we want the recipient of our envy to stub his or her toe? Or worse? We need to place the situation in perspective and try to be rational about our feelings. For starters, let's recognize the extraordinary diversity in all our lives. As people, we're very different. Some of us are successful in this way, others in that way. There's plenty of room for both. Envy is a warning. We need to find out why someone else's recognition or success bothers us so much.

Today I'm going to imagine my life empty of envy. What if I were happy with the life I've made?

What is paralysis but the death of the imagination?

JOHN GUARE

Everybody seems to have moments of laziness and low creativity. Our level of caring becomes low. We cease to be imaginative, fail to take the initiative in life.

At such times we make a mistake if we look at life as if it were a smorgasbord. We assume that we have nothing to do but choose among items before us. We try to believe the hard work of assembling the smorgasbord has already been done for us.

Life isn't like that. We must start from scratch and find what we would like to do. No one else can do this for us: Figuring out what is best for ourself, and creating it if necessary. What is at stake is our happiness and a sense of fulfillment. Failing to undertake this task, we may be locked into a situation that is entirely wrong for us. Such a terrible waste of life is unnecessary. The decision to salvage our life must be our own.

I'm going to reach with my imagination.

Remember, there are many friends in the public library. Books about travel, how-to, and every conceivable subject including people.

Some of our best friends are books. In many cases they're lifelong friends whom we have known intimately for many years. We got acquainted at the beginning of school and went on to share innumerable experiences under every possible kind of circumstance.

The public library is where they make their permanent home. We can roam the aisles between stacks, peruse titles and check authors' names, and choose from the widest range of themes and topics. Within a single hour we may come across adventure stories, histories of nations, suspense novels, biographies of presidents and poets, romance stories, cookbooks, autobiographies of renowned figures, collections of poems, bestsellers, and hidden treasures.

What riches await us. The public library is home for books that we love, so it is a home that awaits us, too.

I remember the last time I lost myself completely in a good book. I'll make the time to do that again.

You lie and hate it and it destroys you and every day is more dangerous, but you live day to day as in a war.

ERNEST HEMINGWAY

It is tragic to view our life as a war and to fight in the trenches every day. This represents an awful waste of infinite good possibilities.

Yet if we set out upon a course of treachery and lies, we weave a web of hate. Then we find ourselves trapped in it. We are so tightly bound that we cannot move. We give up our freedom. Hate is a monster that destroys us day by day. The air we breathe is poisoned. The darkness before our eyes becomes impenetrable. The situation appears hopeless.

It isn't. We can stop the war. Choose peace. Declare a truce. Negotiate new terms. Make a resolution not to lie anymore or be victimized by lies. Stop hating. Take danger in hand and deliberately reduce it to zero. Stand firmly up to what is trying to destroy us and declare: Enough! Now that the war is over, we work for peace.

Today, I'll reexamine my anger and ill will. Is there any other way? I resolve to start looking for it.

MAY 26

I wish I could stop talking about negative things and seeing everything as impossible, adding to my self-imposed misery.

We spend a disproportionate amount of time bitching about what is wrong in any given situation. Sure, something is wrong—always. But there's something right, too.

A positive approach to living is to look for what's right as well as what's wrong. Then, to celebrate what is right, search out possibilities in it, and go to work and act upon them. Why do a number of people find evil more exciting than good? Evil conjures up lurid scenes out of hell. We tend to enjoy these as much as, say, a hot chocolate sundae with nuts and a cherry on top.

When the shouting is over, we're still here and life goes on as usual. We find that positive energy is a lot more helpful than negative. We need to accentuate the positive whenever we can. Give possibility a high priority over impossibility. Say that self-imposed misery is a drag. And stop it.

I don't have the time for misery

I think not only of the places I have been but also of the distances I have travelled within myself.

LAURENS VAN DER POST

Astronauts travel to the moon. Intrepid travelers roam the earth's continents, visit its art treasures and places of extraordinary beauty, eat its ethnic foods and sip its exquisite wines.

Our greatest and longest voyages, however, are within. We traverse valleys, climb mountains, ford rivers, stay, like Marco Polo, in fascinating places for a long time. Some of our voyages take place in our youth, others in middle age, still others when we are old. During them we learn how to test our courage, vitality, and wisdom.

At times an interior voyage may appear to be unprofitable, unrewarding, perhaps even a disaster. Then we learn how to take better journeys. The best brings us to the consciousness of a new world, offering us treasures of wisdom and spiritual bliss. Taking a journey, we never stand still. We're moving.

Today, I'll take some time to look within. It's as vital as remembering to eat.

MAY 28

I am enjoying sex at seventy. The secret we have: I bought two sexy nighties. I have the pink one. He wears the blue one. If we sneak away and elope, I won't be a bit surprised.

Secrets are wonderful. Often they're about things that are nobody else's business. Yet everybody wants to know secrets.

One of the last of our self-governed preserves is our private life. Here, all of us are monarchs, children of gods and goddesses, kings and queens. We're at home in our castle. It's essential that we keep sacrosanct this splendid preserve. Threatening it, the world encroaches upon our personal rights to an intolerable degree.

Our sexuality, a gift of heaven, is a splendid and natural part of who we are. There can be play, succulent secrets, games of the heart, and a relationship between two people that is a hallmark of each of their lives. Having fun is considered questionable by puritans who want to control what everybody else does in body, mind, and spirit. Fun and play constitute a holy gift to humankind.

There's still room in my life for play.

I have a pet raccoon that is lots of fun. He sleeps with the dogs and makes a strange, chirring sound that a damn mocking-bird has learned to imitate, so that we're always thinking Racket is lost in the grove!

MARJORIE KINNAN RAWLINGS

The world of nature calls to us. It's not distant at all. We're a part of it, too. All we need to do is open our eyes and look around.

Much of urban life is, on the surface, a deadening monochrome of cement and glass. Yet when we take a deep look we see birds flying in the air, all sorts of animals sharing life with humans, trees and flowers, lakes and ponds, streams, and wonderful quiet places that allow us to have a retreat amid noise and fury.

We are animals, too. We need our caves and warmth, recreational spaces to roam, earth, food, and affection. Whenever we imagine we are fast-moving robots, hold to a rigid schedule, and deny ourselves time for play and contemplation, we turn our backs upon our humanity. After this we perish in the spirit.

I need the renewal of earth pleasures. I'm going to make the time to walk in a wood, plant some flowers, or swim in a lake.

Certain fears cripple me emotionally and take the vitality and joy out of living. I'm too old to have fears.

Fears crouch inside the various locked closets of our lives. We need to open the closet doors and bring these menacing fears into sunlight and fresh air.

President Franklin D. Roosevelt said that all we have to fear is fear itself. He was right. If we fear darkness, the best antidote is to walk into the dark and find it's safe, even comforting. If we fear another person, we need to unmask the object of our fear and speak to just another human being, not an imaginary source of terror. If we fear water, it's best to immerse our body in it, feeling its healing presence.

Life is entirely too short for us to let ourselves be crippled by irrational fears. They can take the vitality and joy out of our living. They need to be consigned to the nearest dump heap.

Today, I'll face my fears head-on. I'll render them powerless.

I want to keep trying, take risks, keep going, experiment with life, undertake new ventures, and find fresh challenges.

As long as we have breath we can move forward. There is a certain possibility for each of us.

We dare not be self-destructive by giving up. Life is beautiful, a splendid mystery that is our gift. Each day is a new day. To live fully implies that we keep trying. Trying to do what? To choose joy, perceive beauty, reach out, be opened to possibility rather than closed to it, and expect love—even in the face of indifference or hate.

It is exciting to take risks. They open up new windows and doors in our lives, bearing us outside our secret, locked rooms. It is an utterly beneficial thing to experiment with life and play with fresh variations. The lure of something new and original lies just around the next corner. Turn the corner. Accept a fresh challenge.

Today I'll try something totally different. I'll take an unexpected risk. I'll play with fresh variations.

In every older woman you will find a young girl, in every older man a boy.

All of us are people, not just parts of people. Our whole lives are wrapped up in who we are. We're walking stories.

This means childhood and youth are parts of the experience of older men and women. So, when we look at them, we need to see as much of their wholeness as we can. For example, I realize that my ninety-five-year-old mother was once a little girl. It helps me understand her now when I am able to find something of that quality in her, its natural exuberance and laughter, a certain shyness and innocence.

When we meet an elderly man, we should look for the inquisitive, untamed boy as well as the experienced, refined man. When we meet an elderly woman, we should seek to find the girl and the young woman who remain alive as parts of the wholeness of her nature. Perhaps then she can respond to us from these reflections of her past, animating her presence before our eyes.

I won't be afraid to show the child in me.

Duties are what makes life most worth the living. Lacking them, you are not necessary to anyone. And this would be like living in empty space. Or not being alive at all.

MARLENE DIETRICH

Duties are strange things. As kids we often hated them when they involved washing dishes, taking out the garbage, raking leaves, or mopping a floor.

Later, though, duties mysteriously became linked to our being necessary to other people. At work, our duties came to define our identity and relationships. At home, they assumed even deeper meanings when we realized our being necessary to another person is synonymous with loving.

Loving involves others becoming necessary to us, too. A mutual bonding occurs. Being necessary is not all there is, but it's the essential beginning. Whatever our circumstances are, we may opt for caring over selfishness, giving instead of merely taking. Love appears in our lives in many different forms and relates us to a large number of people ranging from a lover to a stranger. It is beneficial to find specific ways to become necessary to other people. This makes life worth living and keeps us truly human.

Today, I'll combat selfishness. I'll make myself necessary, and come through for another.

I just pray that I live at least until my mom is gone so I can see that she is taken care of.

Numerous seers have wisely pointed out that we don't need to go in search of death. It will find us in its own way, its own time.

So, we can't control how long we shall live or when we shall die, unless we take our own life. This means we're unable to make precise plans related to our demise. Many want to live until a child graduates from school or starts a home, a loved one has found security or a parent who is dependent upon our care has departed.

We have no control here. The best we can do is make plans that are as sensible and foolproof as possible. It is a good idea to nurture a sense of well-being instead of anxiety, serenity instead of fear. The projection of negative feelings accomplishes no good purpose and serves to agitate emotions. We can only do our best, give up the illusion of control, and get on with life.

Today, I'll stop trying to control life—and let it be.

The affections are more reticent than the passions, and their expression more subtle.

E. M. FORSTER

How do we express feelings and affection? Some go to the extreme of doing it with a sledgehammer. Others try not to show any feeling at all. Somewhere in the middle between such extremes most of us can be found.

If we can't convey to someone else what we're feeling, a communications gap grows. How can the other person possibly know? Passion sends an unmistakable message, yet it can be scary and threatening if there is not a balance of tenderness and sensitivity.

We show our feelings most significantly in small ways and their repetition. We convey kindness, generosity, caring, loving, and their opposites. Words are not required, but are welcome when sincere. An expression of simple affection is one of the wonders of the world. When repeated again and again, and clearly meant sincerely, it surpasses any treasure.

I'll think about the simple feelings today. I won't let my affections go unnoticed.

After my husband and I retired we were both there for our children—financially, listening to their problems, baby-sitting—until we found we were being used. The only times they called us were the times when they wanted something.

All of us share the need to reach out and communicate with others when we want something. This is natural. But many of us do not communicate nearly so winningly when we don't want anything. This is unfortunate. It hurts other people's feelings. It creates highly plausible suspicions concerning our motives.

Many also take family obligation very much for granted in times of felt need, asking for a blank check, or housing without a time limit, or the total sacrifice of someone else's personal freedom.

To feel we're being used, or taken for granted, can resemble being slapped in the face. It is a jolt. We like, most of us, to pitch in and help others in times of need. We also prefer to be treated as human beings, appreciated, thanked—and called just to say hello or chat.

I'll seek to be appreciated for who I am, as well as for what I can do.

My face looks like a wedding cake left out in the rain.

W. H. AUDEN

We tend to hold a private view of ourselves that may be altogether at odds with how the rest of the world sees us.

Do we find ourselves attractive, handsome, beautiful? Or unattractive, disheveled—perhaps a bit eccentric looking? Do we foolishly compare ourselves with godlike images of youthful movie stars and athletes? On the basis of the standards we've established, we lose.

If we make a comparison between who we are now and who we were thirty, forty, or fifty years ago, what criteria do we use? Yesterday we may have been conventionally good-looking. Today it's entirely possible we possess a kind of strength and beauty that we didn't have in the past, something completely different. Our years and experiences, our sadnesses and joys, have etched lines and drawn shadows on our faces that tell our stories. As there can be great beauty and deep meaning in our stories, so there can be in our faces.

Today, I let my face speak for me openly and without apology.

JUNE 7

I thought when I grew older I would come to golden years, but they are hard years.

No years are perfect in themselves. There is no time in our life that is without problems or boasts only unyielding happiness.

As humans we tend to look forward to a desired state of perfection. Marriage will do it. Childbearing will provide it. Being in love will bring with it lasting perfection. The perfect job will resemble a mythical perfect wave. Creating a flawless work of art will usher in for us an experience of perfection.

On and on we go. The myth of golden years holds that we will bloom like roses in an ambience like Shangri-la, reinforced by wisdom and supported by others' unconditional love. But there is no such time. Always we continue to be faced with struggles, disappointments, losses, and ever new challenges. We can face each new day with fear and dread, or with courage, hope, and the best energy we can muster. The choice is ours.

Today, I'll confront my struggles and losses unclouded by visions of Shangri-la.

Have we—we who have returned—been able to understand and make others understand our experience?

PRIMO LEVI

It isn't enough to live. We have to understand our lives. Otherwise we keep life's meaning away from us.

Our experience is the sum total of where we've been. It isn't sufficient just to have been there. We've got to be able to comprehend it. This involves our taking the time to interpret what we do as we go along. Look around. Take inventory. Share our stories. Recall exact details, what was unsaid, the political posture as well as the personal one, and why did a particular event happen.

In addition, we've got to interpret our life to other people. Have we advanced life's meaning in any way? When? How? Do we understand where we've been, are now, and in what direction we're heading? Only by asking and trying to answer such questions can we help human life advance, make sense of it, and share a mutual purpose.

Where there is meaning in my life, I'll share it with others.

I was born in 1904, the third child of seven. I am the only one left of the family. I have known sorrow and grief, but I think everything that happens is for a purpose

---

Both terrible and wonderful things happen to most of us. Some people simply believe that anything that happens has a purpose in life. Others feel that events are as random as Christmas tree lights.

In my view, anything that happens can have a purpose. We make use of it in creative, caring, intelligent ways. It can teach us a lesson, grant us a benefit. When an event appears to be a tragedy or disaster, it can help us develop perseverance or courage or patience.

To look at events in our lives in sequence—to try to find a meaningful relationship between them—can be profitable. We learn that what had at first seemed to be adversity became an advantage. What appeared to be a big advantage wasn't what we wanted at all.

Today, I see my life as an inevitable progression—everything, good and bad, bringing me to this still moment of gratitude.

Then there is a loneliness that roams.
No rocking can hold it down. It is alive, on
its own.

TONI MORRISON

Loneliness is one of the hardest things we face. It doesn't necessarily have anything to do with other people. Sometimes we can be terribly lonely alone or with others.

A part of loneliness lies in not being comfortable with ourselves as we are. So, instead of finding contentment and peace in quiet moments, we embark upon a course of frenzied activity and distraction. Keep moving! Faster and faster!

Ironically, all this simply increases our intrinsic loneliness. We find to our astonishment that we are still lonely in a crowd. We need to work on our self-acceptance, learn how to find a life within, and achieve a higher level of equanimity that is not dependent on outer stimuli. Loneliness can run treacherously deep, leap out at us from shadows. The best idea is to lose our fear of it, get acquainted, make it a friend.

I'll face my fears of loneliness. I'll reach within for sustenance, and reach out to all who've loved me. I won't be alone

I wonder how many people in the world have died in the last thirty seconds. How many were born? In comparison, how important is my own life?

Statistics can be staggering. I've watched an electric sign on a city building that reported every second the increases that took place in the world's population. It was hypnotizing.

We exist in earth's gigantic space that is filled with oceans, continents, mountains, and nations. Ulysses' journeys took years. Now people fly around the world in a few hours. Outer space offers yet another context. Looking up and staring at a star, it's easy to become overwhelmed by the sheer magnitude and complexity of the view.

We are here, too. At certain moments we feel a certain exhilaration that we are at the dead center of the whole universe. It seems, curiously, to be revolving about us, and our own problems and concerns momentarily block out everything else. Then, in a clearer moment, we realize how limited that view is. Instead we're a part of the cosmos, a vital and living part. Who we are, and what we do, is very important.

Looking at the sun, moon, planets, and stars, I feel a part of everything.

Memories are the specific invisible remains in our lives of what belongs in the past tense.

JANET FLANNER

There are times memories cannot be shared because there is no one left to share them with. Memories are not only in the past, but also invisible, and we can't point to them and explain, "This is where it happened" or "That's the place where we met them."

Memories serve a useful function. They enliven us. They help keep our life resilient, our imagination vivid. However, our memories are not all pleasant. Some are bearers of illumination and beauty, others bring up humiliation and loss and sadness. The combination of these keeps us in touch with reality.

We need to be careful with memories. We can never be absolutely literal about interpreting them because we may recall events differently from the way they actually occurred, especially over the passing of many years. We've changed. Our memories change, too.

I honor the past tense of my life, remembering fondly, and giving thanks.

What staggers me is the shortness of life in comparison with all the things I want to do, places I want to see, people I want to meet.

Life can seem short or long, depending on the circumstances.

We waste too much of life, especially when we're listless and bored instead of being energized and challenged. It's important to want to do lots of things and look forward to doing them. There is so much great music to hear, literature to read, cinema to see, food to eat. There are so many roses to smell, waterfalls to marvel at, oceans and lakes to swim in, hills and mountains to hike up. So many people to know, understand, experience, and learn from.

When we get tired, feel depressed, and wish to turn away from the world, it's a good idea to focus on something we can do instead. Make contact with someone. Help out where we're needed. Stay in touch with life.

Today, I'll turn my eyes from the calendar and clock, stop measuring—and live.

The summer of my sixtieth year is dappled with sun and shadow. . . . In a way that is reminiscent of my early twenties, I am caught by the refraction from some deep, dark, and tender mirror that deflects the personal toward the universal.

ANNE TRUITT

Life's moods vary in astonishing ways. At times we are caught up in the sharp movement, even the maelstrom, of our personal lives. We can't see beyond it.

The problems confronting us at such a moment are not unlike huge waves, hard and menacing. We wonder if we'll find the strength to survive them. Such problems can be related to love or work, a relationship or health, sexuality or economics. Our feet may seem to be trapped in cement. We're conscious of little else in the world.

There comes a shift. It is a new day. Suddenly we're aware of the universe about us, other people and events, the cycle of nature, life's rituals, poems, and music, and the stirrings of hope.

I'll look into the deep, dark mirror. I'll find hope.

JUNE 15

Older people have seen too much, been through too much, to be surprised by anything.

After we've lived many years, it's obvious that we've seen and experienced a great deal of life. Are there any surprises left?

Yes. Fortunately, they never end. We can be surprised by a wide assortment of things including rain, sunshine, betrayal, trust, hate, love, new neighbors, old neighbors, loud noise, a movie, a book, taxes, and death. Surprises provide zest and dash to living. They mean that we're never able to take anything for granted.

It seems to me, in fact, that the older we get, the more surprises there are. Presumably, we've grown so sophisticated and knowledgeable about life, we shouldn't be surprised by anything anymore. But we are. Oh, we are.

Today, I'll welcome a surprise. It's essential to being alive.

Grandma always said she loved me, but when she died I was left out of her will. She left everything to other children and grandkids. I'm furious. I could have used some of her money to help me get started in a new venture.

Perhaps the final way we can express our wishes, and exercise whatever power we may have, is by means of our last will and testament.

Since a will sums up what we want to do with our life's possessions, some people restrict the recipients to family members. Others cut out family and remember favorite causes or charities. Surprises are found in a number of wills. Strangers or little-known people who had never seemed important turn out to have been very, very important to those who died.

Being left out of a will doesn't mean not being loved. Being included in a will isn't necessarily a sign of love at all. Wills are unpredictable, strange, often emotional, more often just businesslike. When we draw up our own will, we should remember it gives us an opportunity for loving—and expressing exactly what we mean by that.

I'll aim to express myself forthrightly and avoid evasion, doubt, and meanness of spirit.

Despite my years, I'm playing hardball with the sun, tennis with the moon. I'm having fun.

We make a big mistake in imbuing age with dignity and solidity when we leave out play and having a good time.

Many men and women missed out on happiness earlier in life. They were forced to take on heavy responsibilities, sometimes to suffer emotional traumas. A delight of age is that it affords an opportunity to recapture lost joy.

Old age can mean cutting through a Gordian knot of stress and finding new outlets for expression and creativity. For many, the entire concept of self-realization and enjoyment was considered highly questionable when weighed against the seemingly unyielding demands of the work ethic. Yet this overlooked the richness and promise of our humanity. We have a constitutional right to the "pursuit of happiness" as a basic tenet of our national heritage. From a spiritual perspective, it is a much needed balance in our work-oriented lives.

I'll look for the source of joy in my life today.

JUNE 18

My grandmother has Alzheimer's disease. I just found out. I have to tell her, try to make her understand, and convince her to leave her lovely home and move into a nursing home which can take the proper care of her.

A catastrophic number of older women and men have, or will develop, Alzheimer's disease.

Yet more is being learned about how to detect and treat it. An enormous mobilization of effort and funding is needed, along with ever increased public awareness, understanding, and knowledge. It is ironic that at a moment in time when AIDS strikes so many who are young, Alzheimer's strikes so many who are older. Both require top prioritization by government and health authorities.

When Alzheimer's comes into the life of someone whom we know and love, it requires all our stamina, commitment, determination, compassion, and love. No one is immune from potentially being touched by it. Alzheimer's is not an isolated disease that affects only a small number of individuals. It is universal in its scope, a health problem of the first magnitude in the ways it can reach out and affect our life.

Whatever happens to one of us, happens to all of us. I'll try to face even the worst with patience and compassion.

As I regard it in my twilight years, the universe is a red bird that sits on a bough of a tree and looks at me.

There are numerous ways to regard the universe. One is to look through a telescope at Saturn and Mars. Another is to listen to a baby's heartbeat.

Many see the universe as out there somewhere. Others believe it lies within each of us. Where do we find the center of meaning? Perhaps in someone whom we love, our work or profession, or an unrealized dream. This becomes a highly personal matter. We may find it difficult even to try putting it into words or explaining it to someone else.

Yet we do see the universe in our own special way. It's related to how we define life's meaning. It grows out of our life's roots and experiences. In the classic film *Citizen Kane* the single word *Rosebud* was found to encompass the mystery of a man's existence, his deepest feelings and motivations.

How do I see my universe? What would be my *rosebud?* I'll look for the symbol of my own life today.

She is climbing her own mountain, in search of her own horizon, after years of being absorbed in the struggles of others.

GERMAINE GREER

We make a mistake when we become involved in the struggles and lives of others to such an extent that we are not true to ourselves at all.

It's easy to become swept away by the expectations and needs of others, especially within a circle of family or friendship. Our entire life becomes enmeshed in someone else's work, happiness, pains, and goals. We lose our sense of identity and forget what we need and want.

This can lead to a situation where we find we are strangers to ourselves. What's wrong is that we've led someone else's life, not our own. Now our life beckons. This may be terrifying if we are out of touch with who we are. It becomes necessary to do some hard homework. We have to find out about ourselves. Then, we need to let significant others know that the change in our life involves them, too, perhaps far more than they ever imagined. It's time for change.

Today, I'll make myself a hardy mountain climber, in search of my next horizon.

JUNE 21

Even though I'm older and have had experience with panic, I just collapse when everything seems to fall apart. It makes me think of a hurricane or an earthquake.

Panic is a natural reaction when the roof is about to blow off or the walls cave in. We are transfixed by terror. Survival becomes our primary, immediate goal.

Emotional upheaval is just as demanding. The ground we stand on is shaking. Our support system appears to be failing. An unexpected disaster has struck. Hope seems far away. What can we do?

As soon as the wind dies down and the shaking ceases—the violent emotional eruption has lost its immediate intensity—we need to see if there is anything pragmatic and rational that we can do in the interest of survival and sanity. Then we need to center ourself, realize we're still here, and figure out what is essential to do next. The moment has come to let go of panic. Now the question is: Where do we go from here? How do we get there?

When panic threatens, I'll center myself, deal quietly and sensibly, and think about what is essential in my life.

go where the action is

it's anywhere

SISTER CORITA

So often the right place for us to be is right where we are. We've overlooked it, maybe because we yearned for distant exotic shores. How attractive they can be as figments of our imagination!

Staying home doesn't mean that we can't make changes. We can. In terms of our own life we can put on a new roof, paint it, start a garden, fix the pipes, wash the windows, and add a room if we like. If this is the best location, we don't have to go halfway around the world, or next door, to find it.

This is a lesson for people who always seem to look elsewhere, never satisfied with what they have at home. There's no perfect place for any of us. Any place will have flaws, raise problems. Are we blind to the possibilities in our present situation? Are we willing to make needed changes?

Today, I'll concentrate on what is right and good in my life, resisting change for its own sake.

JUNE 23

Good-byes, I find, are hard.

It isn't easy to say hello or good-bye. Each requires a definite action on our part. Each calls us to involvement with other people.

Good-byes happen at leavetakings. From home to go to school for the first time, from home for what may be the last time. We are departing en route to somewhere else. Shortly, the present will be the past. What are we leaving, and in search of what? Perhaps we are exchanging security and comfort for risk and raw new adventure. Who knows? We might not even see again a person to whom we're saying good-bye.

Hello can also be terribly risky stuff. If addressed to a new person in our life, does it mean that our life will undergo change? Will we ever say good-bye to the same person? A greeting that signifies change is a symbolic act. We're saying, in effect, that we welcome change and are willing to go with it.

I won't linger over farewell. I'll focus on new meetings. But I'll seek meaning in both

And looking into open graves was no pleasanter than it had ever been. Brown clay and lumps and pebbles—why must it all be so heavy. It was too much weight, oh, far too much to bear.

SAUL BELLOW

When we refuse to look into the sober face of reality, we delude and betray ourselves. Believe me, our view can't always be a fast-paced scene out of a TV sitcom, with a laugh track and in living color.

Ideally, we can have both reality and fantasy. A balance. We prevent this, however, when we repress what threatens to disturb us, want only the laughs, and seek an unreal life. Yet, in reality, there is no such thing as an unreal life. What we repress is bound to show up in painful moments of recognition when we're vulnerable and unprotected.

Better we should decide that we wish to face life honestly, and strike the best balance we can. At least, this is not denying the truth or looking the other way when something happens. And, there's a bonus: When we do this, our laughs are more real, too.

I'm ready to face the harsh truth. I've done it before and survived. I'll look it in the eye, and then move on.

I love children and older people the most.

We can't, in the framework of our human life, manage to love everybody. It's impossible.

The more specific we are about whom we wish to love, the more we're able to love in a universal sense. We have to love someone in order to express our love of everyone. If we say we love everyone, but don't reveal love to anyone, we've fallen into an abyss of contradiction.

Whom, then, shall we love? I suppose whom we really and truly do love. To begin, we have inner circles of family and close friends. Reaching out, we may come to categories of people, not just individuals. For example, some prefer women, others men. Maybe Brazilians or Italians, Lebanese or Kenyans, Chinese or Irish. The favorite people of some are children or older people. The important thing is to express our love of people by starting with the love of a person. Let the love grow.

I'll express my love for one person today and make it hold all the love I feel for life itself.

The longer I lived the more I understood that there were really no lies.

ISAAC BASHEVIS SINGER

Generally we become wiser about life as we grow older. Our understanding should mature along with tolerance for the foibles and shortcomings of other people. When this isn't the case, and we become harshly judgmental and intolerant, we need to heed the danger signals and change.

If we grow mellower, we give others more leeway, consideration, and freedom. Something else happens, too: Little things that used to irritate us gradually seem far less important. We're able to empathize more with other people's feelings, comprehend their pressures and temptations.

As the film *Rashomon* portrayed several varied and conflicting responses to a single event, so we can become open to different views and interpretations, willing to weigh them against our own. We act more sensibly when we learn how to withhold rigid judgment upon others and attempt to figure out why people act the way they do.

Today, I'll move slowly, and not rush to judgment.

JUNE 27

I work in a nursing home with elderly residents who have physical limitations and declining health. Some live with constant pain and loneliness. How can I show them that life is worth living?

We always convey messages about life's meaning to others, whether we're aware of it or not. We do this simply by our attitudes, actions, and beliefs.

So, if we wish to convey the idea that life is worth living, the only real way is to believe it ourselves. Then the idea communicates itself. If we don't believe it, all efforts are doomed to failure.

It's important to realize that people who suffer pain are very, very sensitive about receiving messages. Much of the charade of life has been stripped from them. They have been forced to deal with realism. They are intuitive. With them, words are not nearly so effective as body language, attitude, and actions. Only when we believe that life is worth living can we reach out to them with that message.

I'll live as if life were worthwhile. I'll make it so.

He felt an immense relief. It was as though, after what seemed an interminable time of anxious waiting in the anteroom of death, someone came to him with the good news that he had never expected to hear.

GRAHAM GREENE

What a delight it is when the shadows fall away, clouds vanish, and there is a time of near absolute clarity accompanied by an unexpected companion, good news.

It is all the better when the good news formerly seemed as remote as Outer Mongolia. We did not have any idea it would ever get here. Now here it is, bright as a penny.

We wonder: Is it possible to prepare for such a moment? Consciously await it, month after month, year by year, and do everything possible to be ready? Or is it best to be nonchalant, innocent, unprepared, and open to a surprise that may come our way? I believe that we need to know what good news we yearn to hear; anticipating it increases the pleasure. It is also a splendid idea to give up control and be open to a surprise.

I'm waiting for something good. I'll strive to know it when it comes.

I kept wondering what to do with life. It seemed such a mystery. Then I decided to live.

We can look at our navel and ponder the mystery of life up to just a certain point. Then it's time to act.

Acting isn't hard because all the world's a stage and nearly everybody wants to do it. It's a great group exercise. Better than remaining passive and staying out of it forever. If life's a treat, enjoy it. Sure, we might get burned, but what's wrong with a little fire?

Most of us commit to life. It's a lot different from navel gazing. The mystery of life loses a lot of its glamour when we're working our butt off for something we believe in. This can range from raising a family to working for civil rights, building a business to acquiring an education, composing music to taking self-improvement very seriously. We work and sweat, interact with others, and believe in something. Life is real, and we're living it.

Today I put aside the mystery—and live.

JUNE 30

Brother! Does this look like a face that's been lifted?

BETTE DAVIS

Pride is an indispensable quality in our life. Of course, it can be misused when false pride rears its ugly head. But pride itself is healthy and the life's blood of high self-esteem.

Lots of people and numerous life situations continuously whittle away at our pride. Aging itself is frequently seen as something awful. So, if we move more slowly, someone hellbent on racing like the Indianapolis 500 criticizes us for being an obstacle. If we try to be helpful by citing our own experience in a given situation, someone else finds us egotistical. In other words, we can find our pride under attack from unexpected quarters.

We have to stand up for our maturity, dignity, and rights. We're no more perfect than anyone else; we're also no less perfect. Pride is terribly important when it stiffens our backbone, fixes our clear gaze, reminds us that we're maturer as well as older, and keeps intact our self-respect.

I'm proud of my life and who I am in this moment.

JULY 1

After living so many years my head feels like a haunted house. I have so many ghosts.

It's easy to let ourselves become obsessed with a constantly recurring recollection or thought. Dwelling on it, we allow it to enter into our whole being. Slowly, slowly, it takes on the power of the unforgettable.

If our head feels like a haunted house filled with ghosts, we can do something about it. Open up the windows! Swing wide the doors! Fill the haunted house with air and light. Clean out closets and dark corners. Sweep away cobwebs. Scrub floors. Empty useless old objects out of the attic and cellar. Apply fresh paint.

Letting the sunshine in, we can allow the ghosts to leave. It isn't at all hard to do. What is required is determination, making a decision, and following through. Ghosts don't want to remain anymore because they don't feel at home. Our house is no longer haunted. We're free.

Today I'll set my ghosts free.

There are always openings, if you can find them, there is always something to do.

DONALD BARTHELME

Life, by its very nature, is never closed. It contains openings, even if we have great difficulty locating them.

Since they're there, however, we should never give up the thrill of looking. Some are not conspicuous. Author Sam Keen identifies holes and empty spaces, interstices, pauses, and voids. Openings abound! If our naked eye takes in only great vistas and immense spaces, we're missing the point altogether.

So, we need to ferret out openings we never dreamed of. We may need to start using a magnifying glass. Certainly, our task will require patience. A corollary is that we may wish to find something to do in a place where we had decided there was absolutely nothing to do. All this requires fresh vision and, more specifically, a new focus. Instead of always looking for a new scene, we will deliberately turn back toward an old one, trying to see it in a fresh way.

I'll take a close look around me today. There are fresh openings, and I'll find them.

JULY 3

There are not enough hours in the day. I sew for my grandkids. I have made a garden with cabbage, beets, squash, okra, corn, tomatoes, and beans. I am now canning.

It is a blessing to be fully occupied in a way that satisfies and provides meaning for our life.

Physical activity is great for us when it fits this scheme of things. We can see the results of our labor. What we do benefits other people who feel grateful as well as better for what we did.

A balance between activity and reflection is a good thing, too. Working in a garden can provide it. Whenever we're keeping very, very busy it's advisable to structure times when we can meditate. This lets us stand back from what we've been doing and see it within a larger perspective—our life. Meditation can sound scary and threatening to people: How deep within myself must I go? What if I get lost there? We need it because it's a way to bring balance into our life so that we can alternate between times of busyness and activity, on the one hand, and quiet reflection, on the other.

I promise myself some time close to the earth today. I'll work and reflect—and take strength.

He could figure out everything the easy way,
but he couldn't figure out anything the hard
way, and he didn't like figuring out everything
the easy way and not being able to figure out
anything the hard way.

WILLIAM SAROYAN

Some people understand, and live strictly according to,
the rules. Seemingly they can read correctly all the directions and signs that come into their view.

However, this doesn't mean they understand. But
they confuse the rest of us. They appear to grasp meanings even when they do not. They never—never—reveal
when they're completely lost.

The vast majority of us are vastly confused by the
endless deluge of so-called information that attacks us. It
lacks nuances, shadings, and ways to interpret it. Rules
are much the same; they seem to be written in an un-
translatable code. So we don't understand what's happening to us on many levels: environmental, economic,
military, spiritual, sexual, governmental. We'd like to understand. We'd like to know how our lives are being
shaped by forces that remain either invisible or in disguise.

I'll look for meaning in unexpected places today.

I want to let go of past sorrows.

Some of us tend to collect past sorrows as if they were treasured objects of glass hidden away on a shelf.

We take them down from time to time, touch them gently, and have a good cry. This one might be a sorrow related to an old romance, an affair of the heart. That one is connected to a life's dream we had once. If we had brought it to fruition, our life today would be very different.

While it's valuable to understand where we've been in the past, it is futile to relive decisions made a long while ago. We've changed since then. Our lives became what they did. Perhaps we need to quit regarding past sorrows as sorrows at all. They are things that happened to us. We learned from them. Now it's time to put away our glass menagerie, that sad but foolishly treasured collection of past sorrows. It belongs to the past.

I honor the past, sorrow and all—but today I'll look ahead, expecting something better.

They are remembering together, dreaming together. They can already see it, the walk up the mountain, that time they were so young, when they believed their lives lay ahead of them and all good things were possible.

AMY TAN

I wish we could always believe that all good things are possible. Isn't each day a fresh opportunity? Doesn't every moment carry within it the potential of a new revelation?

Always, our lives lie ahead of us whether we're in kindergarten or retired! Who knows what may happen? We may die at nineteen or live to be ninety-six. While we're still alive, we're open to whatever life may bring us—and what we decide to bring to life.

If we shut down on hope, and decide good things are not possible, we deny the force of change. We die prematurely to our spirit. We consent to be entombed as if we were a Pharaoh, complete with food and drink. Instead we need to seize the new day with a vision of hope, look for indications of good things, use our mind to think up fresh possibilities, and know that our life lies ahead of us until it is over.

I'll recapture the anticipation of what lies ahead. I won't die prematurely in my spirit.

A fruit's ripening is natural and beneficial. It reminds me of aging.

Some older people are startlingly beautiful women and men. Their spiritual inner beauty is a revelation.

I think immediately of a couple whom I know. She is eighty-seven, he is eighty-three. It is one of life's rewards to be with them for a while. They are wiser than Socrates, have the liveliest sense of humor around, maintain a remarkably high level of interest in life, and convey a sense of joy in being together.

Such people are our best teachers on growing older. They show us how to resist a tendency to turn inward. Theirs is an example of how to embrace the world fondly, become interested in the lives of other people, listen intently, counsel patiently, and accept a mentoring role. The more we do this, the more others will want to come to us, share their thoughts and feelings, and be real friends. It means practicing unselfishness, appreciating life, pacing ourselves, and being truly interesting people whom others seek out.

How have I "ripened"? Today, I'll look for my wisdom, and share it.

I peered through the darkness. My lips wanted to form words; I wanted to tell somebody I wanted to be somebody.

PIRI THOMAS

We all want to be somebody. But forces are often at work to dehumanize us, cut us down to size, deny us grace and freedom, and try to destroy our God-given right to enjoy a full life.

Sadly, it's not enough to ask for what belongs to us. Politely, hat in hand. To ask for what is our right is unnecessary. Having to ask is demeaning. What we must do is gather our energy, take a stand, and claim it.

There's even more, however. We can act like we're somebody. This changes us. It lets us be a role model for ourself. Of course, at the same time we're presenting a very different self for others to see and react to. So, we move from being victims and beggars to becoming self-healers and agents of change. When we change, everybody and everything else can change, too.

Today, I reclaim myself. Could I ever have doubted it? I am somebody.

After forty-two years of marriage, the situation just became such that I could not live with it anymore. I moved out of our home, rented a small apartment, continued with the job I love, and have made a very happy life for myself.

Sometimes decisions loom on the horizon like a tidal wave. They force themselves upon us.

Some are complex and hard. We end a relationship, leave a profession or job, move to a new place where we don't know a soul. Wouldn't it be easier to be placed on the rack? Our happiness and well-being seem threatened. We're risking everything with no reward at all in sight. Looking out our window, the view is bleak; it's icy and cold and we're scared to death.

However, we may find happiness beyond our imagination once we've made a clear decision, taken risks in stride, and moved forward. We can't know until we do it. Our attitude is very important. Just to stand still is out of the question, anyway, because we're changing all the time. So is everyone and everything else.

I won't be afraid to make a move. I'll consider my decision, and then I'll stride ahead.

He was an old man, pleased that after a lifetime, with the help of his sons, he had built a solid, well-made house.

V S. NAIPAUL

A sense of accomplishment is one of the great feelings in the world. It answers the question: What have I managed to achieve in my life?

There are vastly diverse ways to measure achievement. Building a pyramid would top some lists, creating a family others. But it's tough when we look in vain for something that we can call an achievement.

Yet maybe we try too hard and even miss the point. In our age of publicity, we tend to look only for big symbols and overlook things on a smaller scale that hold deeper meaning. I believe our most significant achievements include the love we've found and given in life; how we've expressed caring, justice, and hope in our world; a significant difference we managed to make in someone else's life; any redefinition we provided about life's values as we interacted with others; and where we stood for what is right.

What are my real achievements? Where does my satisfaction lie? Today I'll think about what I've done, and what matters.

It makes me sad to think of all those who died young and never got to know old age.

We've all known a wonderful young woman or man who died at an early age, and broke our heart by doing so. Departing so soon, this person seemed without an opportunity to fulfill a life of promise.

Yet who can clearly define life's promise? I believe it cannot be measured by years. Some people live more vividly and deeply within a brief but glorious period of time than others seem to do in a long but less eventful one.

The lesson to be learned is how to live as fully as possible within whatever span of years we have. It's tragic to ever put off living up to our finest potential. It's absurd to assume we'll have endless time. We can assume nothing at all about the amount of time we shall have. It is not a bad idea at all to live today as if it were our final one. Live it to the hilt.

The quality of life is far more important to me than the quantity.

While Pearl Tull was dying, a funny thought occurred to her. It twitched her lips and rustled her breath, and she felt her son lean forward where he kept watch by her bed. "Get ..." she told him. "You should have got ..."

ANNE TYLER

We shouldn't put off until tomorrow what we can do today. Nor is it wise for us to delay telling others what we have to say to them.

Yet most of us walk around with dozens and dozens of unsaid words, sentences, and paragraphs locked inside our heads. We say: "I'll tell her later what I really think." "It would hurt his feelings if I told him the truth." "I never explained to her why I felt she would fail." "We all liked him, but he had a habit that disturbed us, it grew worse, we never told him, but we had to let him go."

It wouldn't be a bad resolution for any of us to start telling the truth—more resolutely, without fear, as a gesture of concern and love. We do incalculable damage to others when we smile pleasantly, refuse to tell the truth, and walk away.

I won't wait to tell the truth. I'll tell it today.

I'm a cute, feisty, li'l old lady with white hair who hasn't let her age and widowhood keep her down. I think other people perceive me as open-minded, flexible, friendly, fun, a little outrageous—and likable.

The difference between how others see us and how we see ourselves can be fascinating. When we think we're being generous, others may find us stingy. While we say we're humble, others might say we're overbearing with ego to burn. The same disparity extends to our appearance, work ability, spirituality, and how we get along with other people. Have you ever been shocked to see a photograph of yourself taken by someone else?

It's a good idea to build bridges between our self-evaluation—how we see ourselves—and how others see us. The wider the gap, the more we might be out of touch with our own reality. We can get significant pointers about ourself from people who are constantly around us. Maybe we've either evaded the truth or been unable to cope with it.

How do others perceive me? How close is that to the way I would be seen? Today, I'll think about how I can honestly make these one.

Retire? What could I retire to? What else am I going to play with?

DUKE ELLINGTON

We draw too long a line between work and retirement. We tend to treat the matter as if it were all or nothing at all.

It is enormously problematic that we do not build enough relaxation, alternative creativity, or pleasure into our work lives. There is too little time for figuring out what it means to be human. Our collective nose is too close to the grindstone. Tough schedules become cruel taskmasters. We run to keep up with deadlines. Suddenly, we seem to have turned over our life to some force that is powerful and alien.

So, it's important to build some aspects of "retirement" into our work life, elements of "work life" into our retirement. It's silly to remain frustrated and unfulfilled in both. Hopefully, we can enjoy parts of each, find meaning where we least expect it, enjoy companions on the common journey, and construct a life that we want.

I'm going to narrow the line between my work and play. I'm going to look for the satisfaction in both.

The mailbox has become my bright spot in the day. I get lots of letters because I write lots of them.

A surprisingly large number of older people write lots of letters. This is especially true of homebound people.

It is nice when the mailbox ceases to sit there as an impersonal receptacle and becomes an integral member of the family. It has room for cards, notes, and letters of every size, in every color. Letters are a great way to reach out, touch other lives, disseminate information, and start friendships.

When we're alone or ill, letters take on an entirely different significance. They are lifelines, bringing joy, greetings, and expressions of caring. They seem to be providential gifts. We should never take our letters, or those of others, for granted or treat them casually.

What treasured friend have I ignored for too long? I'm going to pick up my pen, and write with my heart, *now.*

By a merciful provision of Providence, youth, like death, is something that can only happen to you once.

JAMES GOULD COZZENS

It's a bad mistake when older people think the present generation of youth is going to hell in a handbasket, and when youth reacts by thumbing its nose at seniors.

It's sad when communication breaks down disastrously between the generations. Then, each blames the other for all sorts of things. Seniors may say youths are irresponsible, vain, lazy, immature, and destructive. Youths may say seniors are too set in their ways, prejudiced, cantankerous, out of touch with the present, and refuse to lend a helping hand.

Older people and younger people are all people, after all. Older women and men were once young. Probably they were criticized, too, for being lazy and irresponsible, and thought their seniors were selfish and out of touch. The cycle comes around. We should stop it, get acquainted, and reach out with mutual help.

Today, I'm going to look for the youth still inside me. I'm going to value that spontaneity with all the wisdom of my years.

I am retired from a good job and if I ever feel lonely or depressed, I sit at my easel, pick up my paint brush, get out my paints, put some of the beauty I see on my canvas, and time begins to fly.

Blessed are those who know how to use their hands to make something useful or create a work of art.

Too many fret and stew, hour upon ghastly hour, not knowing how to entertain themselves or fill up the time in constructive ways. This happens whether they're alone or with others. But, if we're working with our hands, our solitariness or gregariousness becomes irrelevant. We're busy. We're doing something. Time seems to move along at a fast clip.

If we don't know how to use our hands, we can learn. Take a painting class or start one in sculpture or gardening or cooking or writing or playing an instrument. There are myriad things to learn how to do. We can take a closer look at activities engaged in by our friends and acquaintances. A whole new world of activity from a totally fresh perspective awaits us.

Today, I'll remember the pleasure I've taken in creating. I'll make the time to do it again.

JULY 18

The trouble is that as I get older, I get more and more interested in beauty. I want things to be beautiful.

CHARLES CHAPLIN

Accompanied by the familiar melody of "September Song," life starts to wind down. Certain things become more precious as awareness grows that time will run out.

Earlier in life, necessities tended to crowd out special interests. It was felt there must be an emphasis on establishing roots, making money, finding a home, launching a reputation, finding a worthy cause for the nurturing of our conscience, and pursuing professional outlets. Often time did not seem to allow undue introspection, reflection, confronting existential questions, or savoring the world's beauty.

However, growing older, we can reorient our life, reprioritize values, wind down certain interests and commence new ones. We may also rediscover old yearnings and passions within us that we denied earlier. Now there is time. An old vision can be resurrected, a lost continent within ourself explored. New life, new interests, beckon.

I have the time to savor beauty. Today, I'll think about what's beautiful in my life. I'll actively pursue it.

JULY 19

Many elderly people are prisoners in their own home to keep out of danger and trouble. You see, old people are fair game to knock around.

Predators represent danger to people who are particularly vulnerable, including children and older women and men.

It is foolish not to take every possible precaution for our safety. We need to lock the doors and windows of our home, avoid walking alone on a dark street and avoid carrying much money, know where we're going and how to get there, acquaint others with our comings and goings, take no chances, stay alert.

Having done all this, is there more that we should do? Yes. We cannot succumb to fear. We have a right to go out anytime we like. Although aware of danger, we must not let local Hitlers rule our lives or bully us. They must know we are not fair game to knock around. So, we have to be utterly sensible and not take obvious risks of any kind. A good rule is to be with others when we are outside. Watch carefully. Be firm.

I'll move carefully and sensibly through my world— but I won't be a prisoner.

The old man's thoughts went on laboriously.
They were leading him nowhere: they doubled
back on themselves and ran the same course
twice: yet he was so accustomed to them that
he could not stop.

T. H. WHITE

Our minds become memory banks, great storing places for thousands of impulses, happenings, actions, reactions, faces, shadows, dreams.

Each of us is a gigantic think tank, analyzing events, reliving moments, trying to make correct sense out of things, telling and retelling stories. Then we try to string together disparate parts, even weave tapestries to integrate them into a whole.

What is probably most important is how we achieve an overview that is objective, and reflects truth, something more than a labyrinth full of our distorted desires and feelings. We need to seek, and be able to find, the light at the end of the tunnel. Our goal should be to know what is true. Ultimately, maybe we can see how we honestly fit into the overall pattern of life, our own and that of other people.

I won't be bound by habit in my thinking. I'll struggle to keep my thoughts free and open.

I'm the resident Grandpa at work, where I've been for thirty years, because I know I have two choices: I can go in complaining or else greet everyone pleasantly.

God knows, all of us have things to complain about from time to time. And we do.

The problem is when other people reach a point where they can't stand our complaining anymore. Sometimes we don't know when to stop. Our griping and whining turn into a bad habit. We move into overkill, lose our sense of humor, and become a deadly bore.

How do we feel when others continually bellyache, find nothing good anywhere, and vent their frustration and anger upon us? It is healthy to express feelings, name demons, cry out for justice, and stand up for rights. However, it can be unhealthy when we want it all our way, cease to respect the feelings of others, refuse to look at someone else's point of view, and keep shouting so loudly we can't hear what another person is trying to say. We live in a world with other people. We can get along with them or make everybody's life miserable, including our own.

If I make every effort to be pleasant, will I find others more pleasant as well? I'm going to find out.

She stands up.
I stand up. "I feel seventy—and I feel twenty."
"I feel a hundred and ten."

DAN MCCALL

It's a funny thing when we try to apply a certain age to our feelings. We all do from time to time. So, one day we say we feel twenty. Another day we comment to someone that we feel seventy.

What is it we're really feeling? It's mood, the weather, metabolism, a dream last night, our digestion, something that someone said, a story in the newspaper or on TV, or the way our breakfast was prepared. Anything small or large influences how we're feeling right now.

This is one of those days we feel twenty, whether we're twenty or not: Early bright sunshine, warm breeze, a bird singing in the distance, a sense of belonging and warmth. And this is one of those days we feel considerably older: None of the right pieces seems to be in place, everything has gone wrong, there is a misunderstanding, gloom pervades as if we were in a lifeboat on the high seas after the sinking of the *Titanic*. But let's quit pegging our good or bad days with age references. Age has nothing to do with it. Moods do.

Today, I'll try feeling the age I am. I am grateful for my maturity.

I am a gay man of seventy-four. My friend died of a heart attack several years ago and unless I find someone else I love as much, he will not be replaced. I keep busy playing music and composing.

None of us ever knows how our life may be changed by something that happens. It is necessary to make our peace with the givenness of life: a death, a separation, an ending.

At the same time, it is vital that we do not place a bolt on a closed door of our life. We may later wish to open the door again; it may simply be opened for us. To make up our mind with finality that there is no new possibility waiting for us is a mistake, because it can appear without warning at any time.

When a door has closed for us, and no new possibility has revealed itself, keeping busy helps make us flexible and saves us from fixating on a painful loss. Busyness is not enough, however. We should strive to maintain openness to serendipity, chance, and possibility. It's good for us to be ready for changes whenever they make an appearance on our doorstep.

There will be endings in my life. But there will always be beginnings. I embrace both.

Moral of my fifty-first birthday: Unless one has learned to work when one is happy, one is no worker. Unless one has learned to work in spite of extreme unhappiness, one will never accomplish much.

GLENWAY WESCOTT

Work can seem a curse or life's greatest blessing. It can be hated or loved, a source of agony or fulfillment, an unfriendly place or a friendly one to be, something we desperately wish to stop or an activity that provides energy and inspiration that we want to keep going.

Or, it can be a combination of these. Work takes up a major portion of most of our lives. It seems absurd to be imprisoned in it, existing in an environment with emotional bars holding us in. It is futile to let decade of unhappy work follow decade of unhappy work.

We should make every effort to discover who we really are and what we really want to become. This is the root knowledge necessary to determine what we actually do. Our work should excite us, uplift us, amuse us, energize us, challenge us, provide us new companions and friends, and bestow upon our life fresh sources of meaning.

I won't let happiness or unhappiness shake me from the work I love.

In some other countries the older population is looked upon with respect and honor. I don't believe this is true in the United States.

Prejudice against older people is like prejudice against African Americans, Latinos, Asian Americans, Native Americans, women, gays and lesbians, handicapped people, and kids. It occurs when somebody seemingly feels a need to dislike or hate someone else, and finds an excuse by stereotyping.

Older women and men in the United States have many advantages, yet prejudice is often directed against them as a group. Some people seem to react angrily at the sight of white or gray hair, the very look of being older. Others object to older people moving slowly or driving a car more slowly. Possibly they are threatened by their own innate fear of growing older. Or they feel that older people stand in their way economically. Often they're rude.

Honor is accorded to few groups of people these days. Yet it is given to particular individuals who earn it. A high proportion of these are elderly people.

What is there in my life worthy of honor? I'll claim it.

I had suggested one day that she might want to write the life story of her grandmother.

PHILLIP LOPATE

Intergenerational relationships are of primary importance. A grandparent has so much wisdom and experience to share with a grandchild. A grandchild can reach out to a grandparent with youthful energy, idealism, and a fresh vision.

A grandparent's message can say there is a family history. Everything is not new; lots of people contributed to our getting where we are. We can learn from women and men in our lineage who showed courage, honor, love, and steadfastness in situations that utterly challenged them. An important lesson of history is that, in understanding it, we don't have to repeat it.

A grandchild's interest and gratitude can provide deep meaning to a grandparent's life. It can be made clear that all that work and sacrifice did matter, after all. Someone who understands will continue what was begun.

Today, I'll recall the grandeur and strength of my own grandparents. I'll write down what I remember. I'll make a record of these heroic figures.

New friends are very hard to make as I grow older. I have been rejected many times. Thank God, I do have a few longstanding friends.

It's hard to define friends. They just are. Friendship is mysterious because it is seldom logical on the surface. While our friends can be so utterly different from us, still they're close and supportive.

Most of us have had certain friends for many, many years. It can seem forever. We grew together in lots of ways, shared innumerable experiences, and know one another intimately. We love such friends more than we like them at particular moments. There is a deep level of trust. Support in time of need is guaranteed.

New friends need to be developed, too. However, we grow lazy, wondering if we have the necessary time and energy for such an awesome task. We may be less prone to begin a new friendship than mourn one that has passed away. Yet a true friend, new or old, is integral to life itself.

When was the last time I made a new friend? I'm not too old to do it again.

He sensed that something terrible was about to happen. He did not know what it was or when it would happen, and he took no comfort in the explanations offered him from all sides.

ABDELRAHMAN MUNIF

Out of ancient history Cassandra lives today in our collective memory as someone who predicted disaster, and was right.

Yet prophets of doom remain in our midst who are wrong. We listen to their shrill prophecies with irritation, a touch of pity, and a wish that they'd go away. Then there are well-meaning people we know, not accredited prophets of doom, who never seem to have a glimmer of hope, a kind word to say, or a moment's peace.

This is a hard way to live. It's also hard on everybody else. If something terrible might happen—although we don't know what, why, where, when, or how—the sensible thing is to avoid hysteria, refuse to create a self-fulfilling illusion of disaster, and live fully the next moment, the next day of life. We can also picture something wonderful about to happen. It just might, especially if we want it and work for it.

I'm going to walk out today expecting something good. I won't be a sucker for doom.

Look, if a man asked me out it wouldn't necessarily be to dance in my mascara, or even necessarily to stay up all night. Maybe he'd love nothing in the world better than to fall asleep in my arms at nine-thirty.

The so-called simple things are what most of us want. Yet we like to deny it, play fire with images of glamour, and give other people the wrong idea of what we want.

Part of the problem lies in our own insecurity. What would someone else think of us if we took off our mask and showed our naked face? Would others laugh at us if they knew we wanted an honest hug instead of a trip to the moon?

Our vulnerability makes us sensitive, so we wear a mask in order to protect ourselves from possible hurt. We keep running in the same futile circle. But if we know what we want, it's self-destructive not to share it with others instead of living a lie. Maybe nobody will laugh at us at all. We can find what we want by sharing our feelings with others.

I'll take a good hug over a trip to the moon anytime.

We can no longer even talk to one another.

WILLIAM INGE

One of the most terrible things in all the world happens when people become so embittered and enraged that they cut off communication by words.

They continue to communicate, of course, by means of the same bitterness and rage. Their body language speaks with the fullness of a dictionary's compendium of words. Hostility and pain become the common language of the day.

Healing can happen unexpectedly when it catches bitter enemies off guard. They've become so locked into their Attila-the-Hun–like roles that all they've done was react to one another. If they are given something else to react to, they may do so. This may lift them outside the context of their emotional imprisonment, even involve them in caring for someone else in need. It may be a way out of the pit of hatred. This might be welcomed by open arms. The haters may be tired and bored and fed up with hating.

Above all, I will keep talking, communicating, and caring.

I would rather be dead than look like a homey, frizzy white-haired Grandma in a house dress, holding a cake.

Why are we so threatened by the way other people appear? Why are we so cruel to them?

I think it's because we fear a part of ourself that, for some inexplicable reason, we see in them. Maybe it's a part of self that we don't want to acknowledge or want others to perceive. It embarrasses us. We don't like it or know how to deal with it.

So, our way of denying our feelings is to strike out against someone whom we think resembles that part of ourself we're rejecting. It can get complicated. But what we're doing is grossly unfair and also absolutely futile. We need to bring the disliked part of ourself out into the open, share it—and accept it. After that, we no longer need to project our rage at self onto other people. The rage is gone.

I'm going to celebrate the uniqueness of other people, applaud their diversity, and simply enjoy knowing them.

AUGUST 1

The old folks are all gone. They were tired, prepared and they went on. Life goes on. Nothing diminishes it. We have been taught also that life is a fragile thing. Grandma always said that it almost feels too good to be alive.

BEVERLY HUNGRY WOLF

If we don't feel good about living, something's wrong. We're missing the point.

We can't live partially. We can't live a little bit. Life requires that we give ourselves fully and completely to the act of living. When we don't, life becomes a farce, a charade, a mistake.

But the exuberance of life can shake us loose from complacency. To be alive, to grasp what that means, produces a sheer riot of raw momentum and bright shades, bracing energy and infinite stillness. What a gift. From the very center of life emanates emotion and feeling. Nothing stops life. We need to throw off any shackles that hold us prisoner and restrain us from living. Life is too great to be treated indifferently, shabbily, or marginally. To honor it, we live it.

Too good. Today, I'm going to try and enjoy life *that* much.

I feel old, helpless, and rejected. I love my daughter, but she won't talk to me or answer my letters.

All of us like the feeling of being in control. So it's painful when we can't be. It's downright maddening when a wished-for letter or phone call is denied us.

Worse, we may not understand why someone is treating us this way. It's natural to overreact, become angry or even obsessed, try to force a showdown, demand an explanation.

However, this ignores what the other person is feeling or thinking. We don't know. If we assume we know, that's just an assumption. In truth, the other person may be busy or preoccupied; ashamed and unable to deal with guilt feelings; furiously angry; unable to communicate with any clarity; totally unaware of how we feel. After the passing of time, a perfect explanation often emerges without any fanfare. What is required of us? Patience.

I'm not going to let life treat me like a leaf on a storm-tossed tree. I won't let my emotions be manipulated by chance.

But, as I was saying to the landlord only this morning, you can't have everything.

DOROTHY PARKER

We find ourselves in a deep pile of trouble when we over-reach, receive no satisfaction from all we have, and try to be Alexander the Great and rule the whole world.

While it's great to be ambitious, it's greater to establish boundaries that are sensible and workable for us. Don't mortgage our life away by buying Buckingham Palace if we can't afford it. Don't try to impress people with our money and prestige, while we're driving them away because we scare them and offend them.

I guess we all know some folks who covet the whole earth and want Mars, too. Sadly, they're usually pretentious, self-preoccupied, boring as hell, overbearing, and we ask: Who needs it? Hopefully we can get a message through to them that they could be likable if they rewrote their act and forgot Mars. As for ourselves, we need to take an occasional reality check and offer thanks for what we have.

What would it take to make me happy? Am I really so far from having all I need? Today, I'll think about the life I *have*.

AUGUST 4

When I was fifty, after many years of marriage and three children, my husband finally admitted he was having an affair. Unfortunately, he was unwilling to give her up and the marriage was broken.

There's an ancient story about a king by the name of Canute who walked down to the seashore one day and ordered the waves to cease.

Like King Canute, we can't exert power over forces of nature or life. There are things we'd like to change that we can't. There's a big drought and we need rain; beating a drum won't bring it; we wait. Someone falls in love with someone whom we consider to be the wrong person; we can't do anything about it.

When unwanted things happen to us, we need to ask ourself the question: Where do we go from here? If we must adapt ourself to a whole new ball game, let's start adapting. If we're going to have to start over, let's get started. It only adds to pain when we become fixated on a situation that we cannot change. It's best to move as forthrightly as possible into a new set of possibilities.

I'll start from here to the place I must go.

AUGUST 5

Well, wasn't that a nostalgic time for me. To walk on that set and be greeted with open arms! He looked fit as a fiddle. He was bouncing in and out of his chair. Frankly, he didn't look a day older than when I'd last seen him, seven years ago.

GLORIA SWANSON

It's important for all of us to have moments of appreciation, drama, revitalization, high energy, and feeling awfully, awfully good.

Life can seem drab when we fall into a routine that goes round and round like the marker on the face of a clock. We yearn for a break in our unchangeable rut, something unexpected to inject a note of surprise and throw a grenade into everybody's plans.

We need to stay open to surprises, and recognize them. A letter may arrive, one we hadn't dreamt of receiving, that contains the most astonishing message of appreciation from someone whom we thought was indifferent. A visit may occur, one that shatters our routine, carrying bright vivacity into our life. We have the capacity to give such a moment to someone else, not merely to receive it.

I can live a long time on one unforgettable moment

I am sixty-six years old and had a constant loving companion for thirty-four years. Since her death, sometimes I think I just can't go on.

The loss of a loved one can be terribly painful and difficult. The very structure of our daily life undergoes a profound change, the familiar becomes unfamiliar, and we are lonely.

We need to realize that a loved one who has departed does not want us to be hurt. How can we avoid it? We will mourn for a while; it is a completely natural reaction to what has happened. Then, out of respect for the loved one, we must pick up the pieces of our life and move forward.

The best way to do this is to look ahead, not backward. Knowing our loved one wants the best for us, it behooves us to cooperate with life. This includes our seeking interaction with other people and new directions of life. These things do not lead to forgetfulness. They beckon us to a renewal of life's energy.

I can go on. I will go on.

AUGUST 7

An odd thing about Merrill was that he seemed unaware that people came in different ages; he was just as likely to ask a nine-year-old to mix him a drink as he was to, say, inquire of an elderly lady what she thought of a character on a kiddie show.

SHEILA BOSWORTH

One of the best things that ever happens to me is to be treated as me. Not as someone old or young, good or bad, male or female, famous or anonymous, rich or poor, employed or unemployed, rural or urban; just me.

Frankly, it doesn't happen often enough. Many people who come into my life obviously have an agenda, see me as someone who can be useful, and stubbornly see their image of me—instead of me.

The occasional person who comes into any of our lives, and relates to us in simple honesty and acceptance, is a marvel and a delight. We need to practice treating others in the same way. To see and accept a human being, without the baggage of labels. Any of us is a walking collection of labels of one kind or another: ethnic, racial, sexual, geographical, or the label of age. It is an inestimable gift to see any of us, first, as a human being.

Today, I'll try discarding labels when I confront other human beings. I'll sit back and enjoy the response.

Self-pity sneaked into my life again when I wasn't looking. Help!

Self-pity is a hydra-headed monster. It reaches into every part of our life. When we become too self-absorbed, we forget to share our life with others and remain open to helping them.

We fail again, and blame it on mom, dad, school, God, politics, that time we failed an exam in the sixth grade, and the time Uncle Louie got drunk before our high school graduation. Oh yes, we can find plenty of reasons for our failure. The world was never kind to us! We were doomed from the outset!

There are reasons for self-pity. We've been hurt badly in the past. We didn't receive the recognition we deserved. Someone cut us down instead of building us up. What are we going to do about it now? Learn how to accept thanks and recognition, feel adequate instead of inadequate, and seek encouragement.

I expect goodness and wonder. I don't have time for self-pity.

The path to holiness is only profane if it is seen as a means to an end. But for us, the end is only as holy as the least holy of the several means we employ.

LAWRENCE KUSHNER

We hear so much about "making it" in our society. It's also called "winning" and "coming out on top."

But often we lose our soul in the act of establishing superiority. Oh yes, an end result may appear good in itself: winning an election or an athletic contest, making a successful business bid or commercial sale. What, however, was required of us?

Did an athlete use steroids in order to gain an edge over a competitor? Did a candidate use dirty tricks to pile up a bigger vote in an election? Did a developer endanger public health by concealing the existence of a toxic waste dump at a building site? The question also comes down to us. Are we willing to cheat or lie, exploit or cover up the facts, to gain an advantage? How much do we care about telling—and being told—the truth?

Today, I'll think about how I'm getting there, rather than where I'm going.

I survived a divorce, a single-parent family with two sons who rebelled at the broken home, a former in-law who has been the blight of my existence, an unplanned retirement, and illness. Life goes on, and we can only give it our best shot.

Life can resemble a soap opera. At times it seems that it might at least be preferable to turn it into a grand opera.

So many things happen to us. They pile up like falling snow. We become confused and feel like a car that's been banged up or an ocean liner about to sink on the open seas. What more could possibly happen? We wait, and bam!—something new threatens our equanimity. How long, how long?

Eventually, the school of hard knocks teaches us how to duck the worst punches, dance around the ring, and store up needed energy for the next round. Sometimes this is called maturity. It is accompanied by a seasoned sense of humor, an overall view that's called perspective, and pluck for the lucky who survive.

How have I survived adversity before? What was it that got me through? I know I can do it again.

I am prepared to meet my Maker. Whether my Maker is prepared for the ordeal of meeting me is another matter.

WINSTON CHURCHILL

How prepared are we for our life to end? Each of our lives will come to a close. Some will do this peacefully, giving us plenty of time to prepare for our demise. Other lives will end violently and without warning.

We tend to read obituaries in the press with considerable detachment, never quite accepting the fact that ours will be there in print one day, too. When a close friend's return from a trip does not occur according to schedule—he's not here! she's not here!—instantly we suspect there's been an accident, and maybe our friend has perished. However, we still give the appearance of believing it won't happen to us. Our *Titanic* won't hit an iceberg. (Of course it will, or else we'll say our good-bye quietly in our own bed at home.) It seems a sensible idea to prepare for our departure now, even as we deal forthrightly with life and strive to become a better person.

I'll live today as if it might be my last—savoring what's good, storing up energy, and meeting fresh challenges.

AUGUST 12

When I'm reading, when I'm really absorbed in a wonderful book, the sort of pleasure I feel is ageless—it occurs in a kind of dreamtime where the me who's reacting never changes. It's the only fountain of youth *I've* found.

One of the things that never changes, whether we're sixteen or sixty-three, is our completely free participation in the imaginative and fascinating world of books.

When we're young we discover the mysterious land of Oz with its Emerald City and yellow-brick road, life twenty thousand leagues under the sea, and we're able to accompany Alice to Wonderland. Once we've shared these experiences and others like them, we can never again be the same as we used to be before our discovery.

As a reader at eighty, we're the same literary adventurer-explorer as we were in junior high school. We turn the next page of an engrossing book with a long familiar aching anticipation of what is yet to come. Our eyes still grow wide in wonder.

Today, I'll find a new book and explore it as if it were a strange, compelling continent. I'm the same adventurer I always was.

Take a two-mile walk every morning before breakfast.

HARRY S. TRUMAN

As an internationally known older man, President Harry S. Truman provided a great example for everybody by setting out on a brisk walk at the start of each new day. Surrounded by his entourage, he was seen moving up the street in sunshine and rain, sleet and ice.

Everybody needs to exercise. It's a matter of good health, physical survival, and spiritual and mental well-being. Yet many older women and men obdurately refuse to exercise. Laziness, it seems to me, is a major reason. It requires guts to turn off the TV or put down the newspaper, get up out of an easy chair, and move.

Walking every day is great. Swimming is fine, along with golf, dancing, gardening, tennis, sturdy housework, and jogging. The bottom line is: Do something. Make a resolution to start exercising regularly.

Today, I'll eat sensibly, take a brisk walk, and strike a blow for good health.

As an older woman and a widow, I watch
those couples who need no one but themselves
and I wonder, who's more selfish?

We're all so different from one another. It's amazing.
Some of us are outgoing and gregarious, others shy and
reclusive. It's never easy at all to understand someone
who represents the other side of the coin.

I wonder why we don't help one another more in understanding each other. We can make it very difficult.
Some of us hide our selfishness under the guise of being
either outgoing or reclusive. The latter is more easily as-
sociated with selfishness because it looks like it. So a
withdrawn, loner type of person is usually more easily
targeted as being uncaring.

However, a far more sophisticated kind of selfishness
may lurk beneath an appearance of gregariousness. Here,
an uncaring person can ironically come across as a car-
bon copy of Mother Teresa. We need to look beneath labels, especially self-manufactured ones.

I'm going to try not to judge. I'm going to live
generously, and look for caring and generosity in
others.

I always had the idea that when I was old I'd get frightfully clever. . . . People would come to me for advice. But nobody ever comes to me for anything, and I don't know a thing.

RALPH RICHARDSON

In the classic film *Lost Horizon*, people in a remote part of the world grow very, very old without appearing to age. The leader is an ancient shamanistic figure possessing ineffable grace, innate dignity, superior wisdom, and the highest honor. So, he becomes an ultimate elder role model.

Younger people seem to approach the elderly in one of two basic ways. Either they treat them with indifference or rude dismissal, regarding them as irrelevant, over-the-hill has-beens who stand in the way of progress, live in the past, and have lost their marbles, or they approach them with a sense of awe, regarding the elderly as icons.

The truth is: Older people are like other people. A few are frightfully clever, a few don't seem to know a thing, and most know a thing or two—or three or four.

How have I become wise by living long? I'll share what I know, when asked.

AUGUST 16

It's been my experience (I'm to be sixty-four next month) that the old curmudgeon and irascible pessimist and complainer of either sex is a full-blown version of what that person was at twenty or twenty-five.

When we attend a high school or college class reunion, and meet once again people whom we haven't seen for thirty, forty, or fifty years, often we experience a shock of recognition: Some seem exactly the same.

This initial view obscures the reality of deep and fundamental changes in everybody. No one stays the same. In addition to changes in faces and bodies, there are unseen ones in personality, character, and outlook.

Life, of course, can dim humor and blur optimism; it can also bring happiness beyond our expectations, and a great sense of trust. But it isn't life that is the initiator. Instead, it is our response to what occurs in our life. We are never locked into any pattern on the basis of who we once were. What's vital is who we are now.

I won't be chained to my past selves. I'm who the years and my actions have made me.

"I wish," Tony Burton said, "there weren't so many words, or it may be because I'm getting old that they confuse me more than they used to. Somehow they keep having more shades of meaning."

JOHN P. MARQUAND

There are dozens, hundreds, thousands of things to confuse us. We live, after all, in a global village. A potpourri of ideas, opinions, and personalities is constantly being infused into our lives.

To make matters even more complicated, people frequently use words to convey meanings dissimilar to the words. Who is to blame? Can something be done to rectify the situation?

We need to accept personal responsibility for our words, correlating words with meanings. So if we say "I love you," we need to mean precisely that, and certainly not the opposite. If it occurs to us there are too many words in use, we might use fewer of them, and judiciously. Where words lead to misunderstanding, we can make a more careful selection of our own. When we disagree, we should eschew customary polite protocol and make it perfectly clear we disagree. Understanding is very important.

I'll take what I say seriously. I'll take responsibility for my words.

Another day has passed so quickly. I am growing older, and it scares me.

When we're young, often we want to grow older. When we're older, often we would like to grow younger.

We're not easily satisfied. The grass always seems to be greener on the other side of the fence. In youth we yearn for more maturity and experience, and to become wiser in the ways of the world. But in older age we can miss the zest of youth, the sheer energy that accompanies it, along with an innocence of spirit and an untested optimism.

It's best for us to possess the virtues of both worlds. We have the opportunity. As older women and men, we can take seriously our mentoring role, act on the wisdom we've acquired, and use our experience for the common good. In addition, we can make room for younger people in our life; combat any signs of a jaded, cynical attitude; ration our energy with care; and stay open to the reservoir of youthful energy in the world.

I'm one hour older than an hour ago. I look forward to the next hour.

AUGUST 19

Our parents would sooner have left us out of Christmas than leave us out of a joke. They explained a joke to us while they were still laughing at it; they tore a still-kicking joke apart, so we could see how it worked.

ANNIE DILLARD

Looking back, it's gratifying to remember all those occasions when we were included by other people in life instead of being excluded.

It's always so much better to feel we're at the center of things. It reflects the consideration and kindness of others. Also, it helps us to comprehend what is going on around us. After all, more is going on at the center than out on the edges of the periphery. We feel more secure at the center.

To be really involved, and see how something works, actually enables us to participate much more fully. We're cut out when we're not able. While others can help and make an enormous difference by including us, it's up to us to find out how things work. Then, we can share this with others.

Today, I'll attempt to include others instead of excluding them. I'll give someone else a place of honor.

I can't drive a nail, put a screw in properly, or do anything that requires carpentry. This is tough when I need to put up curtain rods.

We can't, any of us, do everything. We need help. When we share our skills, the necessary work gets done.

It's no longer even fashionable to be omnipotent. Our world is too complicated, divided into all kinds of areas of expertise. Law and medicine are riddled with specialists. It's increasingly hard for us even to be an expert in a single field; it rapidly becomes subdivided.

An essential element of survival is knowing when to shout "Help!" Everybody does it. It holds no shame. And it provides someone else a chance to do something. Self-reliance was fine on the frontier, but it's outmoded today. It's impossible given the complexity of our shared life. We need to learn how to do our thing, let other people do theirs. The age of solitary heroes and heroines is rapidly vanishing. Group action has taken over.

I'll focus on what I know. And I won't be afraid to ask for help.

Dine with Sibyl Colefax. It is rather tragic, since we all feel that it represents the last big party she will ever be able to give.

HAROLD NICOLSON

Things wind down. It's inevitable that they do. Everything shifts, the old withdraws, the new emerges.

It's good to realize that. What it boils down to is a classic situation: "We've done things our way for a long time, now new people are going to handle them their way, God willing." There is a natural progression to this. It seems to be life's way.

But what's our attitude toward it? Do we extend a warm welcome to a new cast of characters about to walk on stage? Are we judgmental and obstructive, or are we open to what's new? We've got a problem if we feel a change in the old order is tragic. We'll be much happier, and make some interesting new friends, if we can say "Welcome!"

I'll stay ready for the next event.

AUGUST 22

I am one of those unfulfilled souls who feels life has passed me by. Deep inside we feel like sad cases of life run aground, left out of the mainstream.

We need to define life for ourself, not accept abstract definitions given us by others. Any judgment about our fulfillment, or lack of it, needs to be correlated with how we define it.

Some people feel they're in the mainstream, others don't. What is the mainstream? It depends on one's point of view. This leads to enormous confusion when we start to measure ourselves according to other people's standards.

Comparing ourself with others can lead to deep trouble. Compared to so-and-so, we may appear unfulfilled. But, lacking that comparison, we're not! Again, a comparison with someone may give the impression our life has run aground. We need to avoid foolish comparisons and define our own fulfillment, our own concept of what's mainstream.

Today, I won't weigh my life against the mainstream. I'll think about value in my own currency.

Sometimes he felt like an ant about to eat an oak tree.

BERNARD MALAMUD

We are sometimes called upon to undertake great tasks that boggle our minds. One of the most demanding tasks of all is to sustain our life gracefully and productively into old age. It is an awesome challenge.

While there are some fine role models of aging, there aren't many teachers. We have to teach ourselves as we go along. There are countless problems: emotional, physical, spiritual, mental, and financial. Growing old is a juggling act.

Yet we have more limited resources than we did before. We must measure out our energy carefully and wisely. Can we do it? Unquestionably. The answer is found in how. Move slowly, slowly, a step at a time. This is going to take time, patience, guts, faith, hope, and love. All these things are here for us. We must have a plan. Hold fast to it. Believe in it.

When I'm overwhelmed, I'll stop, narrow my focus, and look for a new perspective.

People who are aging now came from an era that believed in keeping problems to themselves. They didn't let others know when they were depressed or hurting over money and health problems.

I can remember when my grandmother confronted a terminal illness. I was a teenager. She confided in me, gave me a letter to be shared with others after her death, and told no one else.

Grandma believed in conveying an example of strength. This meant that she seldom confided in others about her problems. Our life today seems very different. In our age of mass media everybody's story is told to everybody. Secrets are widely publicized and considered juicy.

Yet, despite this flood of information about people, our society is indifferent and uncaring when it comes to meeting the needs of many, including a sizable number of older women and men. Unlike my Grandma, these people tend to let others know when they're hurting and in need. But our society fails them when it refuses to listen, remains aloof, and doesn't care.

When I hurt, I'll say so.

We are all part of a huge family. Within the family our acts of caring, insignificant as they may seem, are nevertheless an integral part of a vast network of compassionate acts that are occurring throughout the universe at each moment.

RAM DASS

A friend of mine, hurt and struggling after a bitter divorce, found herself besieged by anxiety and grief. She could not get her gnawing problem out of the center of her life. Soon she began to teach handicapped children how to create art with clay and paints. Becoming absorbed in them, she realized one day she was no longer concerned by her own problem.

We are at our best when we find our real place in the world in moments that are both ordinary and illuminating. They give us grace even as we interact with life.

It is a miracle of sorts when this occurs, yet it can happen anytime. Without warning, the pace of life begins to shift for us. There are no colors flashing or bells ringing, but transformation takes place. We are aware of it, fully engaged, grateful to be so acutely alive.

Today, I'll think about my place in a larger family. I'll look for acts in my life that connect me to it.

I have AIDS and am in my fifties. My main fear is that I will become a recluse. Work—even aggravating and dismal work—keeps me going.

There is a private place hidden away in many of our lives that is potentially reclusive. We find it attractive when we grow weary of repetitiveness, especially when the repetition seems to bring us no reward at all. The only color we can see is a drab gray. We hear no music.

A haunting invitation beckons us: Drop out. Let it all go. We'll suffer no more hurt. Settle for less. Find a quiet oasis of peace. Get rid of all the anxiety and tension.

At this moment we need a lifeline. Why? Because to disappear from life is to reject it. While we're still living, that's the most self-destructive mistake we can make. A good lifeline is work. It involves us in the nitty-gritty of life, keeps us in touch with other people, provides us wonderful things called deadlines, and takes our mind off despair.

I won't give up on life till it's over.

AUGUST 27

Food is our common ground, a universal experience.

JAMES BEARD

Older people have undoubtedly saved more recipes, but all of us like food, preparing and eating it.

We can remember childhood Thanksgiving dinners, the table piled high with traditional dishes; and Grandma in the kitchen cooking a stew or baking bread and her mythic lemon-jelly cake. Remember, at times we took part in the ritual of homemade ice cream, stirring the thickening strawberry or chocolate cream until we thought our arm might fall off.

Food brings together the generations. We share life when we eat food together. Preparing food is unselfish, generous, and loving. Although a meal can be a work of art, it can vanish within an hour. We need to honor the humility to create an offering that will have such a short life. When we cook a meal, affirming our common ground, we celebrate a universal experience in the here and now.

Today, I'll cook a meal for another and make it an expression of love.

AUGUST 28

There must be a man who would enjoy the company of a fifty-one-year-old woman who has to make it happen again. There must be more to life than to sit it out alone.

We can't wait, any of us, for good things to happen in our life. It is a passive attitude that can stand in the way of anything happening.

We've got to be willing to initiate action. Get out there and connect with somebody and make it happen. If there's a job we want, it won't do any good to sit quietly and hope it will come to us. It won't. It can't. We've got to go after it, say we want it, plan on it, talk to people about it.

The same thing is true of a relationship. Waiting alone, wistfully yearning for lightning to strike in the guise of Mr. Right or Ms. Right marching into our life while the band plays, is guaranteed to keep it from occurring. We have to define what we want, make plans, and go for it.

I refuse to sit this out alone. I'll initiate action.

Maude visits two old women—her mother, who is strong in body, dispirited in mind; the mother's nurse, who is ailing but spirited and bright.

MAUREEN HOWARD

The diversity of our human experience is astonishing. It makes it impossible for us to render facile judgments about anybody.

We've all experienced contrasts in ourselves within the span of a single day. At one moment when we're apparently in top form mentally, we realize we feel rotten physically. At another moment, we're tops physically while not up to par mentally. Life can resemble a roller coaster and we're a passenger.

There's the irony of a particular occasion when we feel terrible and someone pops up and exclaims, "You look wonderful." Generally we smile, acknowledge the compliment, realize quietly how absurd life can be. Naturally we want to be at our best in spirit, mind, and body. When one is momentarily not up to snuff, it's helpful to know the others are doing just fine.

Today, I'll look at my well-being on several planes—spiritual, mental, and physical. I'll make each serve the others.

AUGUST 30

Six years ago I buried my twenty-five-year-old son who desperately wanted to live. Now my eighty-year-old mother is causing me stress, havoc, and much anguish because she wants to die. I can't find any justice or peace in this.

Life holds a mixed bag of surprises, as we all know. Often we cannot find any justice in our situation. However, it's up to us to find peace.

It's heartbreaking when someone we love, who adores life and lives it to the hilt, perishes in an accident or dies slowly of an incurable disease. It's agonizing when someone we love, who has pulled back from the dynamic of life and wishes fervently to die, lives on and on in excruciating pain or emotional despair.

The dilemma, in all its irony, lies outside the bailiwick of our power to change it. Our attitude, however, is up to us. We can't wish reality away. We have to accept it, decide we won't let it destroy our life, and find peace in acceptance.

Today, I'll acknowledge the unpredictability of life. I'll accept what I can't change, and work on what I can. I'll look for peace in acceptance.

Today's dances are horrible! Everybody looks like a spastic scarecrow. Dance floors look like they opened a can of worms. Whatever happened to the fun of touching?

GINGER ROGERS

Different generations tend to see a number of things differently.

Some people living now were born into a world without TV, automobiles, airplanes, supermarkets, movies, and many other things we take for granted. The idea of our going to the moon was seen as poppycock fantasy. (Wasn't there already a man on the moon?) When change hit, it hit hard. Fashion shifts radically decade after decade, along with music, celebrity, and the way people choose to play and enjoy life.

We should try not to get locked inside a particular decade, and find ourself unwilling or unable to empathize with people who have a new way of doing things. Always there is the old, always there is the new. A meeting ground between them is energizing, creative, and instructive for both.

I'll welcome the "shocking." I'm alive, and ready to learn something new.

SEPTEMBER 1

I married my high school sweetheart and soon we will celebrate our golden anniversary. But I always thought my sister was the pretty one and I was ugly. Last week my husband said, "I always thought you were the prettiest girl in the class and I still do." Why, oh why, could he not have said that fifty years ago?

If only we could say at all times exactly what we think. There would be far less misunderstanding, hurt, and confusion.

Of course, this has a darker side, too. There might be small wars all over the place. Yet clarity is to be sought in every situation. "Why did she say that?" "Why didn't he tell me that?" "There's something drastically wrong and I can't get to the bottom of it." "If we could all just put our cards on the table, we could work this out fast."

In the tangled jungle of verbiage, many times we fail to pay a compliment that we intend to offer. We swallow a badly needed explanation, one that can clarify a difficult situation. It's too bad when we can't say what we think.

I want to minimize hurt and confusion in my life. I'll speak up. I won't hold back.

"But now I'm an old man," the General said. "You don't think it's worth while to love me anymore."

LARRY MCMURTRY

Love does not belong solely to any particular age. Youth experiences exuberance, wonder, and delight in discovering it for the first time.

The middle years, at their best, celebrate and nurture love. The older years provide a distinct advantage if we wish to combine what has already been learned with new discovery and fresh delight. Of course, love itself is ageless and timeless. As we know, it contains many tastes, smells, strokes, and shadings. It ranges from raw passion to the sweetest tenderness.

It is never too late to love. All that's ever required is honesty, vulnerability, openness to another, and an overridingly strong desire to choose life. Love is healing. Love is gracious. Love is tender. Love is strong. Love is the greatest gift.

I choose the way of love over any other.

When I visit shut-ins, I put a clown's makeup on my face and wear a clown's costume. To feel the love of new friends is a wonderful experience for both.

To bring joy into someone's life is a lovely thing to do. It can take so little effort and reap great rewards.

We should use our imagination when we visit people who are confined to their home or a hospital. Remember, they can't get outside. They need a spiritual light, a ray of sunshine, a bright intrusion into what may otherwise be a drab, plodding, uneventful day. This provides us an opportunity to offer something unusual.

Above all, we shouldn't bring our own problems with us. Leave them at the door. This is a moment to be outgoing, happy, uplifting, magical, energized, and to make someone else feel good. After we leave, hopefully our presence in the room will remain as a sign of lightness, joy, and hope.

I'll play Peter Pan in someone's life and carry a moment of light.

In a place like this, where so many are lonely, it would be inexcusably selfish to be lonely alone.

TENNESSEE WILLIAMS

When we're lonely, we tend to build a wall around ourself and shut out the rest of the world.

"I hurt!" we say. We may feel we've been rebuffed or rejected by others. Or, that others will not accept us if they know us as we are. We're vulnerable and sensitive. It may seem simpler just not to try to reach out anymore.

Loneliness is a desperately unhappy state to be in. I wonder why we forget it can be shared with someone else who is lonely, too. Why do we often overlook this or even run away from it? We say that we don't want to be hurt again. This overlooks the fact that we're hurting now. It seems important to try not to be selfish with our loneliness, hold onto it as if it were a cherished object, clutch it to our breast with even a touch of drama. We can share it instead.

I'll look for a way to "share" my loneliness.

SEPTEMBER 5

My husband at the age of fifty-seven was diagnosed as having Alzheimer's disease. I am sixty-one years old and still enjoy living. My heart is breaking for him and I'm having a difficult time finding my own way in life with a husband in his condition.

There comes a time in the case of a terminal or incurable disease when we must do everything we possibly can as a caregiver, and at the same time go on living our life.

To be imprisoned as a caregiver in a way that kills our spirit and stifles our expectation for life is not what we are meant for. The concept of life itself must always include love of self. Whenever we try to repress this, bottle it up and put a tight cap on it, we find it emerges in other parts of our life with sometimes devastating results.

Love of self is not intrinsically selfish. If it's lacking one cannot really love another person in a healthy way. We'll want to do everything possible for a loved one in a terminal or incurable illness. This does not include the human sacrifice of our own life.

I'll give thought to caring for myself today. I can't sustain others without doing so.

She was not sure whether she had had a
dream just now or whether there was
something she had meant to remember or to
think about that was troubling her aged mind
like a rat in a wall.

JEAN STAFFORD

Forgetfulness touches many older lives. A word eludes
easy grasp; a name; a situation; a past event; or what day
it is.

Usually, it will eventually crop up. We realize then it
didn't really matter all that much. Life continued on its
way, the sun rose and set, and what big difference did it
make that we couldn't pluck a sought-after name out of
the void?

Forgetting is, to say the least, inconvenient. It gives us
pause. We can wish it were otherwise. However, if it seriously bothers someone else, we need to understand that's
their problem, not ours. You see, there's nothing we can
do about it. So, we'll go on doing the best we can. Surely
no one can ask for more than that.

Today, I'll relax with my forgetfulness. I'll accept it
and refuse to be bothered by it.

It isn't easy to discipline a weakened body or a depressed mind, but it can be done. Set your goal to look outside yourself.

There are times when, looking deeply into self, we encounter the equivalent of a toxic waste dump. We've polluted our own environment, that of our own self.

What can we do? Some give up. Others continue a deplorable process of ravaging self-destruction. Others yearn for recovery.

Recovery is available. It involves looking outside ourself. This lets us see a whole picture in which we're a small part. It helps us find others like ourself. We can share stories, give strength and receive it. We come to realize that hope is something tangible that exists. We discover hidden strengths inside us that we never tapped. We recover self-respect. We find we're not alone at all, but that a circle of acceptance awaits us.

Today, I'll set my sights on something or someone else. I won't brood on myself.

My mother is in her late sixties and is becoming a recluse. She refuses to make any sense out of her life, neglects her health, won't learn a skill or work, is running out of money rapidly, and it's driving me crazy. I can't communicate with her because we always end up shouting at each other over the phone. It would be a lot easier if she were dead.

It seems that one of the hardest lessons to learn is that we are unable to live another person's life.

Parents often try with grim determination to live their children's lives: "You *will* do what I say." "I'm going to teach you how to do this if I have to break your neck."

Ironically, children sometimes try to do the same thing with older parents, reversing roles: "*I* know what is best for you." "*Why* don't you behave the way I want you to do?" But the meaning of love includes letting go. A person has a right to his or her own life, without our interference. The closer we are to someone, the more we can try to act like a dictator. Better to be a friend than a dictator.

Today, I give up control of others' lives. I'll do my best with my own.

If unable to be independent as an older woman, I, for one, would like to be allowed, after adequate counseling and a waiting period, to be given a lethal injection or pills, go to sleep, and not wake up.

I remember a hit play in the 1960s called *Stop the World, I Want to Get Off.* It expressed humorously the way most of us feel occasionally when life becomes too hectic.

However, we can't stop the world unless we're Superman. And, when it comes to jumping off and leaving the action behind, it's not as simple or easy as it might seem. I don't believe our life belongs exclusively to us in a selfish way. We're in life with other people. It's a community enterprise. We owe life, and other people, something.

The biggest challenge on earth is reinventing the next day. Honoring it. Loving it. Polishing it and making it shine. Other people need us just as much as we need them. We need to embrace life together.

Who are the people I owe, whose lives would be changed without me? I'll think of them today, and of my value to them.

It's funny about voices, Diana Vreeland still
has a young voice. Strong.

ANDY WARHOL

A number of older people have known the experience of
talking to someone on the phone with some frequency,
then meeting the person. "I don't believe your age," the
person exclaims. "You sound so young on the phone."

Routine judgments about aging, as of virtually everything else, are changing. More and more we realize it's
simply impossible to package people under convenient
labels of race, geography, ethnicity, gender, or age.

We can't generalize. It comes down to us as individuals. Some older people are younger in terms of energy
than many younger people, for example. We'll continue
to look for signs of stereotyping, and be surprised when
they fail, until we learn how to see ourself and other people as individuals.

I won't make age-related judgments. And I'll try to
rise above them when they're aimed at me.

SEPTEMBER 11

After a lifetime of giving, it is now my turn to receive. My family will grow in the process as I find a new life, one more devoted to my own welfare.

Reciprocity is fairness. No one person should give and give and give, and not receive, while another receives and receives and receives.

We've all known an unappreciated giver. Other givers allow an imbalance to grow between their giving and receiving. This can be near fatal. However, an unappreciated giver should not be required to bear the additional burden of asking for a change. Since we're dealing here with a dysfunctional situation, this often happens.

When a change is requested, it may come as a shock to an insensitive receiver who has blatantly exploited the role of a giver. Yet such a moment of truth is significant for both a receiver and a giver. The time has come for someone else's turn. Now a giver can experience what it feels like to be a receiver.

Today, I'll ask for my fair share.

Just as I once loved them, I love them still and forever.

ISADORA DUNCAN

We continue to love the people whom we have loved in our life. This does not mean being "in" love. It means loving with a sense of gratitude, recognition, and belonging. The fact that it's in the past does not obliterate it.

This is one of the solid truths about our existence. The passing of time helps us to remember with affection the good moments, blur the unfortunate ones.

The people whom we have loved helped mold the personality we have today, influenced our thinking, affected our tastes and habits, and introduced us to whole new worlds we would never have visited without them. Some of them we knew briefly, others for many years. Old controversies are dead; so are misunderstandings, recriminations, hurts, and fears. Now these people live on in our lives, our thoughts, our affections.

I keep something within me of all I've loved. This is a part of wisdom.

I am caught in the sandwich generation between my children (whom I have lost all patience with) and my mother (who is absolutely impossible). I am fifty-seven. I thought these years would be my happiest. Help!

If you had thought you could simply retire and go fishing, you were dead wrong. You'll need all the help you can get.

The demands made upon people who are caught between their responsibilities toward children and parents are sometimes awesome. A basic rule is: Don't lose patience. It is a prerequisite for survival.

While we need to cultivate patience within ourselves, there is another need, too. It is to feel patience toward other people in our lives who can't help the fact that they are problems for us. They can never be regarded as absolutely impossible. A far better attitude is *always possible*. We must remain open to a full range of possibility when it comes to the other key players in our life. Remember: Our present years can be our happiest—but only if we make them that way.

My happiness is up to me. Today, I'll work with reality, but look for possibilities.

I opened a dizzy eye part way. So this was heaven—this white expanse that swung and swam before my languid gaze? No, it could not be—it did not smell like heaven. It smelled like a hospital. It was a hospital.

IRVIN COBB

Visits to a hospital are generally not fun and games. They're pretty serious most of the time. And, as all of us know who have stayed there for any length of time, a hospital is the last place on earth to go for a rest.

However, a visit there represents a total change of scene. There is nothing else quite like a hospital. It's a beehive of activity. Dozens of individual dramas are being played out. People are there for a purpose, their guard is down, and communication is earnest.

When all kinds of superficial barriers between people are down, we can get to know someone in a hospital, and be known. Issues are big ones: Health, illness, death, survival, life. None of us will go out of our way to spend time in a hospital, but when we do, it's one of the best learning centers on earth.

I won't be afraid of hospitals. I'll take whatever comfort I can to a sick friend. And I'll look at the other human faces while I'm there.

It's such a mistake to waste time. It's more valuable than gold and diamonds and money.

Wasting time is wasting life. Yet what does it mean to waste it?

Workaholics want to account for every moment, every hour. They believe in keeping busy and working hard. Some may consider it a waste to wander by a seashore, smell a rose, visit an art museum (unless as part of a school course), stop to watch a fountain cascade, or sit around and sing songs.

It isn't. Time exists for us, we don't exist for time. It's up to us what we want to do with it. Some perceive time as if it were a formidable mountain to be climbed, and they treat it aggressively and competitively. Others may see it as a rambling, gently moving stream, and treat it amiably and kindly. How we see time says more about us than it does about time. We should make it a friend, not an enemy. It's not a bad idea to love time.

How am I spending my "valuable"? Today, I'm going to give myself a gift of time, and do something just because I choose to.

SEPTEMBER 16

I shall be richer all my life for this sorrow.

WALLACE STEGNER

Periods of greatest growth in our life often come during pain and sadness. We have to call everything into question. We must decide how to go on.

Such moments are so strong that, in a curious way, they affect the course of our whole life. We learn so much, so fast. Momentarily we're overwhelmed, thrown for a loop, unable to move. Sorrow invades our life. We look for resources to deal with it.

We absorb the pain, gradually place sorrow behind us, and gently resume the pace of living. Life beckons with vitality and colors and new risks. But we're not the same, will never be the same again. We've been shaken. We were wounded. Now we are in a healing process. Having come up against a mighty force, we've survived. We are stronger now than we were before. Our life is richer.

How has sorrow enriched me? What enabled me to recover, and go on? Today, I'll bask in my survival.

SEPTEMBER 17

I have never married and have never been an outgoing person. After my mother's death I looked after my father for twenty-one years until he died when I was sixty-three. I am determined to make the most of what is left of my life.

Each of our lives is an incredible mystery. Each tells its own story, weaves its unique pattern, conjures up a set of different meanings.

None of our lives reveals its deepest truths on the surface. We make the mistake sometimes of pitying someone who has no need of pity, or rewarding someone who deserves no reward. We're working in the dark here. Using outward symbols reflected by a life, we make assumptions and act upon them.

I think the most important thing to do with any life is make the most of what's left. This brings us strongly into the present moment. What's past is gone. The future we do not know. But in the present moment we can harness our energy, gather up our dreams, and aim to make the very most of what remains. While this may sound like an awesome task, it's a realizable one.

Today, I'll ponder the rest of my story. I'll consider where I'd like the plot to turn. Then, I'll begin to make it happen.

"Pop," he whispered, gently taking Father's hand. Father's hands were rather small-boned and slender. Mother had told us we were lucky to have inherited them from him, an opinion that had always pleased him enough to quote. Now his hand seemed like a child's in Bill's.

BROOKE HAYWARD

It's significant when an elderly parent's role reverts to that of a child, in a sense of dependency and needing care, and a former child assumes a parental role in providing care.

This requires as much sensitivity and love from both parties as possible. The parent will, of course, remain the parent; a child will always remain the same in the very structure and history of the relationship.

The old relationship, interweaving with the emerging new one, will inescapably hold mystery and require subtlety. The dignity of the parent must be preserved. So must the freedom of the child.

I'll keep myself ready and open for a changed relationship.

SEPTEMBER 19

My husband and I lived together for forty years. He died three years ago. Most nights I wake up to see him coming down the hall. Sometimes he looks sad, sometimes angry.

Our life can become almost totally intertwined with the life of someone we love.

Year after year we did the same things together, thought similar thoughts, shared food and drink, sex and love, opinions and ideas, hugs and nurturing, joys and friends, disappointments and defeats, travel and our home.

When parting comes, it is devastating. It seems that no one else can really understand the depth of it. A basic part of our self is gone. But then, another part remains. We see our beloved, speak and hear, feel the presence close to us. We will never be alone. We look forward to being reunited in a fuller sense. We are more grateful than angry, content than sad.

I won't forget the ones I've lost. But I'll go on.

A medical revolution has extended the life of our older citizens without providing the dignity and security these later years deserve.

JOHN F. KENNEDY

We're already forgetting how comparatively young many people used to be when they died. Now in our present age people are living longer and longer.

Great strides in improving the welfare of older women and men has been chronicled. Now older people have come to exist in the public consciousness as a group that is valued and appreciated. There's a new interest in our needs, concerns, aspirations, and contributions. Prejudice toward the elderly is neither chic nor generally acceptable.

It's beginning to dawn on an ever-increasing number of people that they're going to grow old, too. They ask: What's to become of them? Where will they live? How will they get medical care they can afford? Who will take care of them? Who will care? The problem has come full circle.

How will I maintain dignity and security in my life? I'll think of what that means, and begin to plan.

I'm eighty and I go to the Senior Center several times a week, take care of my two great grandchildren one day, and deliver Meals on Wheels. These things get me out and I am with people.

We need to get out and be with other people as much as possible. It's stimulating: we can share and laugh and get new ideas.

Meeting friends at a Senior Center, and maybe volunteering to do some work there, is a splendid idea. It's important to see how others are managing with the same sort of needs and problems that we have. There can be an exchange of everything from self-help remedies to suggestions for pen pals.

Staying alone prevents us from receiving needed input from others. We think too much about ourselves, become fixated on problems, and narrow our focus on life. It's necessary to get our mind off what worries us, and onto how other people are feeling, coping, and what is the dynamic that keeps them going.

I won't try to make it alone. Today, I'll give in to my need for other people.

The rich, gentle authority of someone who has experienced most of what he wished in life, was there, heightened by a craggy mellowness and a wheeze with each draw of breath.

AXEL MADSEN

How many of us feel that we've experienced most of what we wished in our life? It depends, in part, on the kind of dreams and yearnings we've had.

In our secret dreams do we want to climb Mt. Everest, occupy the Oval office, star at MGM, or discover the world's richest gold mine? The answer tells a great deal about us. Conversely, do we want to help feed the hungry, provide support for the homeless, assist political refugees, or do volunteer work with youth in the inner city?

We need to set goals that correspond to our yearnings and skills. What do we want to do? What can we do? If we've been on the wrong track, we can alter our route and make new beginnings. It's encouraging to have a role model, to see someone who's managed to make sense of life and is fulfilled.

Today, I'll inspect my secret dreams.

SEPTEMBER 23

I know seniors who can't stop suffering over the loss of a child decades ago, or their parents' divorce back in history. They spend mental and emotional time wishing things could be "put back the way they used to be," no matter how fruitless this is.

Some people can't seem to get over the past. A divorce or a death still haunts them, bringing up great unhappiness and causing distress.

We need to let ghosts have their long-desired peace. They wander restlessly through our life, from attic to cellar, and only we can free them. They disrupt our life, but we hold firmly onto them as if they were an obsession.

To free them means to let them leave at last. They have been imprisoned in our memory too long. Some of them may go back all the way to our childhood. They represent things that we never allowed ourself to resolve or make peace with. The time has come. When they are free, so are we.

Today, I'll make a conscious effort to deal with past unhappiness. Enough! I'll let it go.

He was not a happy person. He couldn't possibly be. His life was too complicated. Complicated to such an extent, so many layers, that he did not really know himself.

KATHARINE HEPBURN

It's a great gift if we know who we are. It also helps everybody else immeasurably.

We're not making sense of our life when we turn it into a labyrinthine Casbah of mystery, complexity, and confusion. Doing this, we're unable to make connections even among the parts of our own life, let alone try relating to someone else. If others have to unfold layer after layer after layer in order to get to us, most will become bored and walk away.

When we're in an absolute mess, can we mold our life into shape again? Some say no. Others argue that it's terribly hard. The truth is, it's much harder not to. The task involves, first, taking a close, penetrating look at our web of complexity. Don't flinch. What do we see? Next, we need to dismantle it slowly, placing the pieces in various parts where they belong. What we're doing is creating a livable space. A breathing space. Our life requires this.

I'm going to keep in touch with my self, and make sure others do as well. By doing so, I'll create a livable space.

Mothers try so hard to be included with their daughters, and it's a losing battle.

The whole meaning of a family is undergoing radical change. One out of three American children is growing up with one parent. Children receive primary instruction from their peers and mass media.

In older days, the family was far more self-contained. Elderly members often lived as integral parts of the family. There could be natural interaction between young and old members.

Lots of working fathers and mothers now have little opportunity to spend much time with their children. Everybody can seem to be on an assembly-line schedule. Slack time is frequently filled by TV. Communication grows harder, not easier. It seems an excellent idea whenever mothers can spend time with daughters, fathers with sons, mothers with sons, fathers with daughters. It's sad when people in a family have to remain strangers, alienated, unable to know one another.

I accept the changing roles in my family. I'll strive to be friend foremost, brother, mother, cousin second.

I keep observing how other people die, comparing, learning, critiquing the process inside of me, matching it to how I would like to do it.

AUDRE LORDE

I suppose most of us wonder at times how we'll die. Will it occur violently in an accident or a crash? Quietly in bed at home? As a patient in a hospital? Alone or with friends? Will we have a warning or will it be a surprise?

I wonder even more about our attitude. Will we be afraid? Serene and accepting? Will we fight against dying? Some of us have been with someone when he or she died, and shared the solemnity and release of that moment. My first experience was at my grandfather's death when I was still a young boy. We're also familiar to some extent with examples of how various well-known historical persons died.

Yet our own death must be our own creation. It's possible that our act of dying will be the single most important moment in our life.

My death is an important moment. I won't let it come without sufficient preparation.

It is not true that life is one damn thing after another—it's one damn thing over and over.

EDNA ST. VINCENT MILLAY

Monotony can be a bore, even an enemy. This is why we strive to find new recipes, clothes, TV shows, alternative routes to drive our car, and faces in the news.

Better, we say, to have one thing after another than one thing over and over. At least we think we can vary our pattern, find some distinctions, get a breath of fresh air.

What we really need is to sharpen our sense of anticipation and make it a point to enjoy what comes to us. We lose sight of what amazing things come down the pike. Unbelievable surprises come our way, both welcome and unwelcome. It's a smorgasbord beyond compare. How silly to become jaded and let ourself be bored. Wait for what's ahead, and get a kick out of it.

I won't be overwhelmed by sameness. It's entirely up to my own effort.

SEPTEMBER 28

Those Texas gals and I really had a rowdy hour and a half. I confessed to them that my bracelet was phony, that I was wearing stage make-up, that my beauty wasn't what it had been twenty years earlier.

TALLULAH BANKHEAD

Pretense gets in the way of so much human contact. We play elaborate games to keep other people at bay, even while we yearn for their company.

Yet we have one big option. We can open up to our games and tell the truth about ourself. It's refreshing when we do. People are initially surprised, sometimes caught off guard, then delighted.

There's another surprise when people know the truth before we tell them. This can make our cover-up games look ridiculous. It also illustrates the kindness of others who accept us even as we play our masquerade. Our lives are open books more than we like to acknowledge. It's as if we were all inhabitants of a huge library with all our books wide open, and everybody casually poring over them. There are very, very few secrets. Sharing truths is an invitation to friendship.

Today, an experiment. I'll try telling three important truths to the first person I meet.

My life was my husband and family. He was diagnosed with lung cancer and in a year he was dead and I felt part of me had died.

We love to have a sense of structure in our life. It can seem like the Rock of Gibraltar, absolutely safe and unassailable.

But the structure can come apart, fall down, and change completely before our eyes. There is never any guaranteed permanence in human life. A death or illness, accident or an unexpected disaster, can topple what appeared to be our security.

When our life changes abruptly, we must be resilient, accept the fact, and get on with living as well as possible. Maybe we'll feel we're not the same person we were because the entire content of our life has been irremediably changed. What is new, even if we can't recognize it yet, is all we have. We must manage to create a new life.

The only surety in life is change. I'll embrace it. I'm still alive.

SEPTEMBER 30

And I thought how small and selfish is sorrow. But it bangs one about until one is senseless and I can never thank you enough for giving me such a delicious book wherein I found so much beauty and hope, quite suddenly one day by the river.

QUEEN ELIZABETH THE QUEEN MOTHER

Sorrow can seem a small, solitary thing, but is far more than that. It can lunge and tear viciously like a large, ravenous rat. It can be absolutely overwhelming.

We don't admit sorrow. It enters itself. It is an unmistakable reality that we must deal with. It's here and won't go away. The question becomes: Do we wish to be its host or victim? It's up to us how we treat sorrow, and how it treats us.

If we cringe and vacillate before sorrow, we've virtually decided to be its victim. On the other hand, sorrow knows when it has met its match in us. Although it won't go away, it will behave and accept our rules.

I'll be sorrow's host, and let it meet its match in me.

OCTOBER 1

Make voyages, attempt them, there's nothing else.

TENNESSEE WILLIAMS

We need to be adventuresome about life, particularly in our maturer years. There is a whole world to be known and explored. While some voyages are taken on ships and jet planes, others are of the spirit.

This means taking off on an uncharted journey: Trying something new in our life, letting a fresh idea stir us, exploring an unknown continent of the interior life. It can involve a genuine risk and even misunderstanding. Someone shocked by our behavior may exclaim, "You're a bloody fool."

But it is a sign of genuine maturity to follow your own heart and decide "This is the time to do it." It's silly to remain a bystander of life instead of an explorer. There's no time like the present. Life is filled with tantalizing mystery. The only way to get to know it intimately is, first, to become involved with it vulnerably.

Today, I'll be an explorer. I'm ready to scout new territory.

Grandmother was rich, and I won't go into this. She was a stout woman with a plain face but the fact that she happened never to have worried about money had left her, even as an old woman, with an uncommon freshness.

JOHN CHEEVER

Money is one of the strangest things. Sometimes it lifts worries, other times it causes and exacerbates them.

Money is like politics, religion, and sex. What happens depends on the use we make of them. Money can become our overseer or our servant. It can help bring us to fulfillment or become a destructive force.

But money tends to bring us more, not fewer, worries. We may desire to hold onto it at any cost. We may become obsessed with the idea of increasing its worth. We may fear others are trying to take it away from us. We may believe we are admired or even loved only because of it. We need to spend it, give it away, and never become its slave, even if we're the richest slave in the world.

I need my creature comforts, but I won't let money concerns line my face.

When I see an elderly bag lady I think: How did she live a whole lifetime and end up alone and without help? It makes me count my friends.

One of the most startling sights on a city street is that of an older woman dressed in rags, with a cart that contains all her possessions, lying on a bus stop bench and covered with yesterday's newspapers for warmth. She needs food, clothing, medical care, friends, and love. What hideous set of circumstances brought her to such a naked moment of decline and need? We cannot discount her as an aberration or some kind of outsider.

Many stand in peril of occupying her shoes someday. Her condition underscores a denial of compassion and a terrible wrong at the core of our society. This older woman lives alone as an alien on our streets. Poor and defenseless, she is a part of our life. She warns us not to let our hearts become hearts of stone.

Today, I'll count the blessings of friendship and support. I'll extend myself to someone lacking these.

I've got to get some seeds, right away.
Nothing's planted. I don't have a thing in the
ground.

ARTHUR MILLER

There come moments in life when everything seems
about to be swept away in a great tragedy, a searing illumination of truth, or a feeling of awful emptiness. All
our illusions of stability have been shattered. Where we
previously felt we were safe, now we are convinced we're
not at all. We may have been lied to, deceived, or swin-
dled. Perhaps we had even built a psychological or physical facade that was meant to shield us from diversity.
Now we realize it's made of papier-mâché, worthless for
the task.

We sense an overpowering need to compensate for
what we perceive to be our loss. We seek genuine security now. No more lies, no more deception, no more loss.
It's time to set our house in order. We realize it's up to us,
and no one else.

Today, I clear the decks. I'll think about what I need
to do now to put my house in order.

OCTOBER 5

My greatest fear is of losing my memory. I'm living for today, but I'm also a sort of walking testament to my dead lover. If I forget his story—the way he smiled—he's just gone, lost.

Other lives are contained in our own. Their stories are interwoven with ours. Their memory rests in ours.

This keeps us going when we might otherwise give up quietly. A lot rides on our shoulders. We need to pass on to new generations the stories we've shared, names and faces, challenges and battles, victories and losses, and the love we knew.

We are most alive when we're engaged in being a walking testament. It takes our mind off our own worries and bruises, letting us share a wider and brighter vision of life. We live not just for ourself, but for others, too. This adds dimension and meaning to our life, making it richer and more purposeful.

Whose are the stories I carry? Today, I'll take stock of that trust. I'll draw on the strength it offers.

People who have been much loved retain even in old age a radiating quality difficult to describe but unmistakable. Even a stone that has been blazed on all day by a southern sun will hold heat long after nightfall; one Madame de Bülow, who was far from being a stone and not yet at the close of her day, had this warm radiance.

DAME ETHEL SMYTH

To be loved is a gorgeous experience.

To be loved, and loved more, and loved even more, is better. How can this happen? It occurs when there is mutuality. We must also love if we are to be loved.

Love is contagious. When we've got it, others catch it, too. We show signs of love in our eyes, on our face, in our body. It's a lovely sign. When we want more love in our life, all we need is give more.

Today, I'll love generously and without stinting. I'll hold nothing back.

I am caring for my mother who is ailing, forgetful, and negative. Forgetful is the hardest because I must repeat, repeat, and repeat. I try to remember that one day I may also be in need and try to do the best I can for today.

To err is human. To forget is a damn nuisance.

Yet, growing older, most of us tend to be more forgetful than we used to be. This means, in practical terms, that it's often necessary for others to repeat what they said. Nothing is intrinsically wrong with that. To repeat seemingly guarantees more grasp of the content. It underscores and underlines.

It's helpful to imagine we're speaking a foreign language when we repeat. It's a language that consists of repeats. So, in order to learn it, we need to repeat and repeat and repeat. No harm is done, it can be a bit of fun, the message gets across, and nobody's feelings get hurt. There's even a bonus. This is good training for us. Our day will arrive when we'll need to hear words repeated. We might as well get used to it.

I may forget things someday too. While I've got the gift of clear memory, I'll strive to be gracious and helpful to those who forget now.

It would affect every aspect of the way we live our lives if we all of a sudden had average life spans of one-hundred and twenty years instead of seventy years.

THOMAS JOHNSON, MOLECULAR BIOLOGIST

Most of us spend some time wondering how many years we'll have to live. But what we might want doesn't usually have a great deal to do with it.

Yet if we had a choice, how many years would we choose? I suppose much of the answer is concerned with health, economic well-being, and day-by-day happiness.

Columnist Ellen Goodman noted that women are not being given permission to age gracefully: "The culture is telling women that they can be younger longer. It is not welcoming old women." Is it welcoming anyone old? How long many of us may wish to live needs to be correlated with how we feel we fit into life, how accepting others are of us, and how natural and relaxed we can be instead of having to play acceptable roles. Are we OK as we are?

I'm going to live my live fully *today*, and let that take up all my time and energy.

I am twelve and live with my grandmother. She drives me crazy. She wants me to act like a lady all the time and just doesn't want to accept the fact that I am not a little girl anymore.

Oh, dear. Somebody needs to let Grandma know.

When it comes to age differences, most of us frequently seem to be driving the rest of us crazy. Why doesn't our grandmother act like a grandmother (and quit embarrassing us?) instead of spinning corny stories and staying up late? Why doesn't our granddaughter act like a granddaughter should—be proper, respectful, and well, a lady?

The problem is this: we're human. We're individuals. We don't want anyone building fences around us, constricting our impulses, holding us in, saying No, repressing our energy. We adamantly refuse to let anyone prescribe "correct" behavior for us that feels like a straitjacket. No! We don't want our growth (at whatever age) to be stunted. We won't be forced into a double standard that makes us act this way while our real self is going that way.

It can't be done too often: today, I assert my freedom to simply be myself.

I have been silent while the great autumn light begins; a time of change in the inner world.

MAY SARTON

We have inner seasons as well as outer ones. The two often converge.

In a cold winter we can be like a bear in a cave, hibernating, staying warm, gathering energy. Perhaps we're an introspective bear. In spring a long, long anticipation gives way to freshness and lightness and brightness and stirrings of ecstasy. In summer we can laze by the meandering river, take the boat out on the water, nap beneath a leafy tree, walk deep into the forest, then sit in a hammock and read a thick book.

Autumn is the most mysterious of the seasons. We feel it deep in our soul. There's a bracing wind, red leaves fall, we seem to be waiting for something to come. Mortality is in the air, along with wisdom and discipline and a different quality of light.

This is my season. Today, I'll take a walk through fallen leaves, and think about what's ending, and what beginning, in my life.

For fifty years I lived happily with another woman. Now she's dead, I'm eighty years old and scared. My nurse has brought me back to the church and made me give up all my "evil" friends. Now I'm lonely.

We have to assert our independence again and again, remaining ever vigilant. There everlastingly seems to be somebody waiting in the wings to keep us from being free.

There are zealots who vociferously declaim they're limiting our freedom for our own good. Why they wish to become self-appointed arbiters of public morality remains a puzzle. Perhaps they were bitterly unhappy in their childhood, and want everyone else to share their misery. They seem to hurt badly when they see a happy face; they don't want anyone to fly. They cast imprecations to bring others down to a level where they can seize their joy.

It's up to us to assert our rights against such misguided, dictatorial zealots. No one has any right to scare us and make us feel lonely or hopeless. No one.

I won't let fear or prejudice narrow my life—not mine, not anyone else's.

To his tired eyes, everything now looked stale. He had, as he often said, used up the world: There was no place that could provide him contentment, no place for him at all.

GERALD CLARKE

One of the wisest things is always to leave new worlds to conquer, vistas to explore, visions to realize.

It's stupid to dry up. We do it when we get greedy, egomaniacal, and want everything. We become like little Alexander the Greats, boastfully running around conquering ever new worlds. We also become boring as hell. Somebody needs to tell us to lighten up, relax, live and let live, give up control, and try to be human.

Some older people fear letting go will mean losing everything, being forced out, becoming irrelevant. The truth is that it's time to shift gears, accept a new role as an elder, rediscover freshness, allow room for someone younger, and discover an altogether new space of contentment and achievement.

Today, I renew my commitment to life. I'll rub my eyes and look on a new world.

There were days when from the moment she came out of sleep, she could feel doom hanging over her head like a low rain cloud.

PAUL BOWLES

Doom can be addictive. What was once feared, ironically becomes something one actively seeks to find.

We need to turn around the awesome power of depression and not allow it to sap our spiritual vitality. How can we do this? First, refuse to be hypnotized by the allure of doom. It's a dead end that represents finality instead of continuity. Second, learn alternative ways to confront doom. Get up. Start moving. Do things that need to be done. Talk to other people—in person, on the phone, or write a letter. Have projects that make time and energy demands. Meditate, reflect, or pray. Literally help someone. Be involved in life. Third, demythologize doom. Laugh at it. See it as pitiful, even ridiculous. It's kid stuff. We don't have time for that anymore.

Addiction is limiting. It is also controlling and confining. We need to free our life from it.

Today I'll walk away from doom. I'm ready for something different.

No one person really discovered me. I was discovered over and over again, every time some director or producer saw a quality he could bring out that I usually didn't even know I had.

MYRNA LOY

We need to see ourselves in the eyes of others. We need the help of others to define who we are, assess our possibilities, and make us grow in directions we never dreamed of.

When we rely on our own instincts and self-knowledge, we limit our potential. Our view of self can be small, distorted, or else grandiose to a dangerous degree. Others can often have a much better sense of who we are. I think we first learn this early in school. Later, others close to us may have a major effect on our life for this reason.

They help flesh out our life. A friend or co-worker may see a quality in us that we're completely unaware of. But until the quality is brought out, it merely remains an unused part of us.

Today, I'll try to see myself from another's perspective. Good or bad, is there something I've missed? I'll make myself open to a different view.

An older person in a state of true
contentment is to be envied beyond all others.

There is something indescribably beautiful about a life
near completion that is incandescent and shines bright.
We can see in the eyes of such a person innocence and
maturity, awareness and forgiveness. It's almost as if the
life were exposed as, say, the trunk of a giant redwood
tree, its course marked by cylindrical cycles.

To be in the presence of such a person seems a blessing. Each word, every gesture, holds meanings. There are
mysteries to be unraveled here, secrets told, wisdom ex-
tracted. Time seems to stand still or else move very, very
slowly; it is no longer in control. Silences communicate
volumes. Fully here, we're also in another country, another realm. We feel life itself is about to be explained
after the next breath, the next moment.

Whom would I consider my elders? Today, I'm going
to look out for contentment in someone older. I'll
think about what would bring contentment in my life.

Thirty years is a long time, I guess, and yet as I come here now to write about them the memories skip about and make no patterns and I know only certain of them are to be trusted.

LILLIAN HELLMAN

All of us revise our own life stories constantly. Conveniently we forget this, subconsciously we revise that.

In our recollection, faces fade, then reemerge somewhat differently from what they were. Incidents take on meanings they never had. We discover significance where there was none, humor where it was lacking, and a merest trace of tragedy where it was actually overwhelming.

This is perfectly all right. After all, it's our life story. We lived it. We observed it through our eyes. We experienced it through our senses. When there's a canvas, we painted it. When there's a book, we wrote it. The ways in which we recollect our life are a part of our own being. Opinions matter as well as facts. Pilate asked, "What is truth?" It is relative and mercurial, often unbearable, strange and mystifying, sometimes unrecognizable, and rarer than the richest ruby.

Today, I'll take up my story and tell it again in a new way, paint it with different colors. It's my story; it's up to me.

My mother's thoughts are turned only to what she cannot do. She speaks only of her aches and pains and the bleakness of her life. Whatever I try to do for her is met with a negative response and nothing is ever right.

Sometimes we have to do our very best against odds that seem insurmountable.

At such a time it seems to us there is only darkness, no light. The weight upon us is unbearable. We cry out for an answer, but hear only more questions. Like Job, we realize that we find ourself in a crucial moment of trial.

We can only place one foot ahead of the other, and edge slowly forward. Our duty seems to call for a repetition of sameness. We receive no thanks, only criticism. We wonder if what we are doing is right. Sacrificing our energy and time, we'd like to feel appreciated. The difficult time extends itself. Then, sometimes there comes a turning, a change, a positive response. It is enormously helpful, and we are grateful.

In a sea of negativity, I'll endure. I'll watch for a turning point or a positive response—and that will be everything.

OCTOBER 18

Old Mr. Marblehall never did anything, never got married until he was sixty.

EUDORA WELTY

We should never be surprised by anyone else's life. We say other people do the darnedest things. So do we.

The point is that we can only read outer signs of another life. Usually we have no idea what is going on inside. Suddenly, something dramatic happens in that life, and we're scarcely able to grasp it.

But something is always going on inside a life: moss grows here, a tree root is buried there; here's a secret cave, there's a pathway up a mountain. Our lives contain so many hidden places. When we seem to have stopped growing on the outside, inner growth remains slow, steady, and strong. This is why human judgments fail. We can't see inside.

What would surprise people most about me if they knew? What am I waiting to do? Why am I waiting?

I am seventy-one and have lost all trust in my husband, who has betrayed me with another woman. We are still together because it is financially impossible to separate. I feel hurt, depressed, humiliated, unwanted, unloved, and without hope.

We are never meant to live at the whim of someone else, no matter how close. Our own life is of inestimable importance.

To feel betrayed is awful. But sometimes there are circumstances we don't fully understand. We may even have contributed unwittingly to the problem in some way. If the matter can be discussed openly, every aspect of the situation brought out, this can prove valuable.

When all else fails, other people may need to enter in, attempting to mediate, seek alternatives, work out ways in which a seemingly impossible situation may somehow become a possible one.

Forgiveness is about forgiving, not about the magnitude of the crime. Today, I'll reclaim what's mine with forgiveness and love.

The son or daughter who takes on the responsibility of caring for an elderly parent is never prepared to deal with the guilt that caring leaves behind.

Caring for anyone is a sensitive and complicated thing to do. It requires endless patience, self-control, and an awareness of someone else's feelings.

There can be drudgery involved in caring. One person is ostensibly in a position of control while the other is not. This can lead to resistance against authority on the one hand, and misuse of power on the other.

Anger can easily come to the forefront in such a relationship, along with frustration, emotional fatigue, and cruelty. The person who is caring must realize that the other is dependent, needy, and not always in command of his or her resources. This is an uneven coupling of people possessing vastly different strengths, weaknesses, and skills. Guilt can follow when we lose patience and give way to emotions that ravage our spirit and hurt the other.

Today, I'll stop and acknowledge the good I'm doing. I'm grateful for my power to do it.

Do not go gentle into that good night, . . .
Rage, rage against the dying of the light.

DYLAN THOMAS

No! This is all wrong. Why should we turn our departure from this life into a nightmare or a bad experience? Why should we rage against death, which is a part of life?

Anyhow, let's get down to particulars. We have no evidence there is a dying of the light. Maybe the light grows brighter, shines more luminously, projects its healing rays into every crevice of our existence. And anyway, rage seems a petulant, knee-jerk, negative, self-destructive reaction. Rage leads directly to alienation and annihilation.

Let's instead go tenderly, gently, and lovingly into what is sometimes called a good night. It may turn out to be a good morning, a fresh and wonderful experience of the soul. Meanwhile, why don't we place rage on a convenient shelf and leave it there? We won't rage against the dying of the light. We will lovingly and hopefully prepare ourselves for what may be our greatest adventure.

Today, I'll let myself think quietly and fearlessly about death.

OCTOBER 22

And I saw your apology in your eyes, under your admirable poise, impressive in an elderly man with little education who had come to see a child he abandoned twenty years before.

KATE MILLETT

How can we forgive on some occasions? It takes our breath away, seems almost impossible. Why should we?

When we don't, we carry more luggage around than can fit into Grand Central Station. We become overburdened, our arms feel like they're about to fall off. Our mind comes near to exploding, too, filled with rage and frustration and hurt.

Can we get rid of all this? Permanently? Countless people say yes. It isn't complicated to do. Actually, it's a simple operation from a logistical standpoint. First, we place all the excess baggage on the ground. Then we leave it there. We don't have to lug it around anymore. We don't have to think about it during the day, dream about it through the night. We forgive, and that's that.

Today, I'll forgive an old wrong, however distant, however long ago. I'll feel a weight lifted.

Sitting in a dark room never solves anything.

Whenever we can, it's good to let the sunlight in. We can see more clearly. Usually we feel better.

Life requires light and movement. Life is an ongoing enterprise. It has a beginning, a middle, and an end. The end conveys a sense of destination and purpose.

When we become immobile, we need to get started up again. Life involves other people. It's not good to become reclusive and isolated. There are difficult moments when we simply run out of fuel, and need someone to walk in and give us a mighty shove. However, we can't count on that. We may have to become a self-starter. This requires our making a decision, screwing up our courage, and making a real move. Don't forget, it's easier to do this in a sunlit room than a dark one.

I don't have time to brood. Today, I head for the light and open air

It's better to be looked over than overlooked.

MAE WEST

At any age we need to keep up, take care of ourselves, and face the world honestly with a smile and our best foot forward.

It's easy to go to pot, give up, make no effort at all, and hide what charm we have. It's also damn foolishness and extremely unfair to other people. Everybody wants a bit of cheer, a dash of color, a touch of style, and a person at his or her natural best.

This requires neither magic nor alchemy. But we need to consent to play our part on the world's stage where we find ourself. We drain something from life when we refuse to be as alert and interesting as we can, enter into the ritual of living, wear clothes that are clean and fresh, go out of our way to greet people, and hold firmly onto a zest for life. Simple dignity and good humor, natural charm and mature grace never go out of style.

Today, I'll make the effort to be noticed. I'll wear my heart on my sleeve. I won't be invisible.

My self-esteem is sinking, yet I know I have strength or I could not have survived as many emotional and physical blows as I have taken.

Life's wounds strengthen us sometimes, weaken us at others. Wounds by themselves tend to be debilitating. Yet they serve to awaken our spirit and courage.

It's foolhardy to seek out wounds as if they were trophies. They can exact a great price. Usually it requires considerable strength to survive them, and heal. So, we need to protect ourself from being wounded as much as possible.

Yet all of us have deep wounds that we live with. To deny them is tantamount to preventing their healing. We need to acknowledge them, share them with others who are close to us, and do everything possible to contribute to their gradual healing. When we can do this, they may become blessings in disguise.

Today, I'll examine my wounds, not with sorrow, but with the pride of a survivor.

I retire when I die. One never knows the ending.

ALFRED HITCHCOCK

It's unarguable that death signals retirement. If we haven't retired until then, we finally do it.

On the other hand, who knows what follows death? Maybe it's not like retirement at all. It could well be a striking new life, a far livelier adventure than this one, an incredible journey into uncharted territory of the spirit.

Despite all the kinds of control we think we have over life, we don't know the ending at all. It's up for grabs. It's a good thing there are still surprises ahead of us. This keeps life interesting. Life unfolds as it wishes, and death is a part of life. So, we keep guessing and trying to do our best. Our departure is a mystery that will be revealed. After that final retirement comes new life.

Today, I'll concentrate completely on being alive in the present moment. I'll wait to find out what happens next.

At sixty-nine I can look back and understand that all my problems were fear-based, nameless fears that caused me untold agony and mental anguish.

We need to deal with fears when they arise in our life, one by one—confront them and try to transform them. When we don't, they have a tendency to gang up on us. It's a dismaying sight to look out and see a gang of fears bearing down on us. Fears multiply quickly, feeding on one another. A climate of fear makes it easy for them.

So, it's smart to learn how to take on one fear at a time. Analyze it. Figure out how it gets to us, crippling us and reducing us to shivers. We need to break the hold a fear has on us. Most fears are irrational. Anything that can terrify us and break our will is an enemy. Our mature lives have no room for this kind of decidedly unfriendly force.

What frightens me? Today, I face my fears head-on, and move beyond them.

How many of us have sought after our rights, while subtly retaining the mistaken notion that we might not be worthy of them?

MARK THOMPSON

Older people have been made the butt of many cruel jokes, subjected to ridicule, and relegated to the dustbin of society by those who are apparently terrified of growing old and don't want to see any visible signs of it.

This has naturally caused a number of elderly women and men to experience feelings of low self-esteem. If anyone is made to feel ridiculous or worthless or below the status of others, the result is a sense of worthlessness. It can take a long time and considerable effort to repair such damage to a human being.

It is essential that we see ourself in the best possible light and affirm our worthiness to all rights and privileges. We must never lose sight of this or allow anyone else to intrude on it.

I know my rights and am worthy of them.

I have learned to live with pain, but mostly it's prayer. One must try very hard to concentrate on other things.

Pain can take over our life. It makes incessant demands. It insinuates itself into every part of our being.

To remove it from the center of our life is a salvific thing to do. But we can't just pick it up as if it were an object, and place it elsewhere.

Our mind and spirit provide the way to remove it. We can learn how to focus the center of our attention somewhere else. It's as if we possess a giant spotlight that we slowly turn from shining here to shining there. Prayer and meditation are excellent ways to change our focus. The point is that our attention turns elsewhere. When it does, we are freed from an obsessive concentration on anything that seeks to tyrannize our life.

Today, I'll look for a good distraction. I won't be ruled by pain.

None of us can help the things that life has done to us. They're done before you realize it, and once they're done they make you do other things until at last everything comes between you and what you'd like to be, and you've lost your true self forever.

EUGENE O'NEILL

We can turn our life around. Reverse a direction. Alter a course. Set in motion fundamental changes within ourself.

This is part of the miracle of living. We never have to be trapped or defeated. Our human spirit is a force of inestimable strength. Of course, it's true that life does things to us. Habits and traits are set in place. Some people go on to self-destructive patterns. Addictions occur.

Yet we never lose the power to choose and make a decision. This power provides reservoirs of energy for us. Once we learn how to tap it, strength belongs to us. Our true self is never lost. Always it is a presence in our life, reminding us who we are, calling us to our own particular greatness.

There was no wrong turning in the path. Only turnings. Today, I'll take the direction of my choice. It lies within my power.

I'll be damned if I'll go around making monkey faces and kissing babies just because I'm old enough to be a grandmother. If they're interested, they can come kiss *me*.

Sometimes we find we've overextended ourself and gone out to the world altogether too much. It's time to pause, change rhythm, and let the world come to us for a change. Then a new balance can emerge.

Maybe it's time to surprise others who live or work with us by asserting a new side of our personality they aren't accustomed to. They can meet a part of us that deserves attention, space, time, oxygen, love—and applause. All this can take place in a new scenario of our life that we introduce.

Change is not only beneficial, but downright necessary on occasion. If we've gone out of our way to please others too much, perhaps we want to do less now to win their favor and instead ask them to support us in a fresh mood. Or, if we've been self-centered and refused to please others, maybe the moment has come to be more outoing, generous, sacrificing, and loving.

I won't let my behavior be dictated by age

NOVEMBER 1

It was winter: November, with late gloomy
dawns and a cold wind smacking the leaves
about on sticky pavements. The season suited
me. Even at forty-one it dawns on one that
one will not live forever. *Adieu jeunesse.*

IRIS MURDOCH

If we're thinking about our mortality—whether we're
forty-one or eighty-one—a cold, windy, rainy day seems
to fit our mood more perfectly than a day when the sun
is shining extravagantly.

Or, if we're madly happy—the world is topsy-turvy
with scintillating joy—it's marvelous if it's also springtime, flowers bloom, the air is like perfume, and the sky
is the most gorgeous blue.

However, since the weather doesn't always cooperate
in blending with our mood, it's wise to cultivate our
imagination. Then, if we face a savage day when a blizzard rages mercilessly, but we feel the need of a warm,
gentle breeze, all we need do is conjure up a picture of a
faraway island. Presto. In a few moments we don't even
remember there was a blizzard. To enter a garden of
one's imagination, one has only to open a gate, and walk
inside.

Today, I'll appreciate the romance of the season
without conceding doom. Farewell youth, maybe, but
well met, maturity.

I have just begun to realize what a terribly dysfunctional family I grew up in. I'm fifty, my mother is going on seventy, and I am so filled with rage at her that I can't stand to see her or talk to her. I detest her and what she did to hurt me as a child.

We make a big mistake when we attempt to look at life in terms of starkly contrasting shades of black and white, period, instead of discerning all kinds of mixed images in subtle and overlapping grays.

Life is made up of gradations instead of absolutes. All of us make mistakes, big ones. We have good intentions that go awry sometimes, and work out very well at other times.

It is self-defeating to designate someone as the enemy, and absolve ourself from any involvement in a bad situation. Unless we can work through our anger and rage toward another person, it is we who suffer more than anyone else. Often a quality that we detest in another person is one imbedded deep in ourself.

Today, I'll look calmly to the source of my anger. Would I live differently free of it?

When he turned seventy-one Henry [Ford] showed up to meet the press wearing two different shoes. Asked about it by reporters, he looked down and, obviously making up an answer on the spot, said that he always wore one old shoe on his birthday to remind himself that he had once been poor and might be again.

PETER COLLIER AND DAVID HOROWITZ

As we grow older, we have a chance to indulge our sense of humor, our individuality, and even to become a bit eccentric if we wish.

Behind us are many years of required conformity, when it was harder to assert our feelings. Maybe there was a dress code that stipulated what we must wear. Perhaps in the workplace there were definite limitations on how much we could express an individual opinion. We had to earn a living, please a boss, play a prescribed role, offend no one, stick around long enough to pick up a pension.

Now, as a senior, we should be able at last to say and do what we like, fully express our individuality, and even cause others on occasion to stand open-mouthed in pure wonderment.

I'll be as outspoken and eccentric as I feel, today and all days.

I'm a fifty-eight-year-old gay man. My life-partner died two years ago. I live alone in the home we shared. Despite having lots of friends, staying exceptionally active, and holding down a responsible managerial position that keeps me unusually busy, I am desperately lonely and worry about what the future holds.

It can be a mistake when we keep running too fast and too hard after we've suffered loss and pain.

At times it's necessary to slow down, accept the solace and deep meaning of solitude, and cultivate patience. This can prove to be very healing.

We can be on a perpetual merry-go-round, with noise and distraction, lots of activism and socializing, yet lose contact with the center of our own life. The center is indispensable for our spiritual and emotional renewal. When we're in close touch with it, we can deal much better with loss and loneliness, and quietly peer at our future with patience.

I won't be afraid of solitude. Today, I'll quit running away and give loss my full attention

When I turn and look behind me, I like to see where I have been.

WRIGHT MORRIS

We need to celebrate our lives. But sadly, some of us harbor feelings of shame and regret, and look backward without joy. It is necessary to see the good as well as the evil in certain situations that were painful and crippling. To accept forgiveness for those mistakes and misdeeds of ours that hurt other people. To forgive others who afflicted us with hurt, brutality, and betrayal.

We need to turn and look behind us. It is a healing, nurturing, healthy thing to do. We cannot effectively deal with the present unless we comprehend the past and view it in a clear perspective. It's important to see where we have been in order to visualize ourselves today.

I won't lose sight of where I've been. It's necessary to plan for and get where I'm going.

NOVEMBER 6

My mother wanted everybody to think that our household was one of unimpeachable dignity, where all human passion was absolutely under control.

MARGARET HALSEY

How practiced most of us are in creating nice images of our lives! We confront the world with them. They make us appear to be always virtuous, strong, sinless, and successful.

They are not altogether lies; hopefully we are at least some of these things. But our images remain fabrications we've painstakingly constructed. They reveal how we wish to be seen by other people, and maybe even by ourselves.

When we force these images before the eyes of other people, we make it difficult for them to know us as we truly are. Nobody can love an image. We force our friends to undertake the laborious task of getting through our image in order to reach us. Why not make it easier for them? Let's concentrate on reality.

Help me to discard my self-constructed image and show my naked face.

My vision of my mother eating at those happy, noisy, groaning boards is of a woman jumping up and sitting down, cutting off bites that she chewed on the run to the kitchen to get more for the rest of us, a woman whose plate always seemed to contain what looked like trimmings and odd pieces and quarter portions, who finished what others left.

MIMI SHERATON

Many of us can remember a mother who sacrificed for us in innumerable ways, often relinquished her share, and sometimes left us feeling both thankful and guilty.

Usually no one else in our life ever comes close to approximating a mother's traditional outpouring of largess. She becomes an almost mythical role model in our memory. Are we supposed to emulate it?

No. Probably it's better for us to be more even-handed in giving and receiving. We can be generous. Yet it may be easier for others if we strike a balance when it comes to bigger-than-life acts of sacrifice. In doing so, we absolve others of feeling guilty or unworthy. We can learn to give and receive more equally.

I hope to give freely to others what I'm able to share, and to accept what's given with grace.

My husband and I played Scrabble every Sunday with a much younger couple for many years. We watched their kids grow up. One day they just stopped returning our calls, as if we'd never existed. I guess we were too old.

An old adage goes something like this: "Everybody is odd but me and thee. And some days I think thou art odd, too."

Human nature is far more unpredictable than the strangest weather pattern can ever be. All of us surprise others at times by our actions. We cause joy and jubilation, hurt and dismay.

We need to realize other people's actions that jolt us are usually not capable of easy analysis. Such actions tend to defy logical, rational explanation. They are buried deep in psychological matter. Since we don't understand, we should avoid making assumptions. A good friend of mine has two words framed and displayed prominently on his desk: ASSUME NOTHING. This comes close to being the best advice in the world.

Today, I stop looking for a reason for the hurts I've sustained. And start healing.

Once, my father gave me a dime—the last dime in the house, though I didn't know that—to go to the store for kerosene for the stove, and I fell on the icy streets and dropped the dime and lost it. My father beat me with an iron cord from the kitchen to the back room and back again, until I lay, half-conscious, on my belly on the floor.

JAMES BALDWIN

Most of us have bad incidents to remember. To deny them, or try to bury them, is a mistake. They'll crop up somewhere else in our life. We need to take them out and examine them, try to understand why they happened, and share them with others.

We must also erase our own feelings of guilt in relationship to them, and see the incidents for what they are. Someone was troubled; someone was wrong; someone wronged others, including us.

When we come to a place where we can finally forgive, we begin to heal. We need to do that for our physical, mental, and spiritual health.

Give me the courage to look back, see what I see, and tell no lies.

I'm an eighty-seven-year-old man. My wife and all five of my brothers and sisters have died, as have two of my three children. What's the point in living when nearly everyone I love is gone?

Life isn't over until it's over. But there are times—we may be twenty or seventy, forty or eighty—when we ask: What is the point in living?

Moments when we ask this question tend to be crucial turning points. We may have had our professional life wiped out or lost a job. We may have ended a marriage or loving relationship, or lost a child or partner in death. Maybe we feel we've run out of steam, have nowhere to go, and can't make it.

So we ask: How can I get from here to there? From today to tomorrow? The middle of the night to the next morning? Sunrise to sunset? At our worst moment everyone we love seems to be gone, along with our own self-esteem, our very faith and hope. But before long something curious happens. Hope beckons. Life stirs again. We realize the point in living is living itself.

Today I start small. I'll make life itself reason to live.

I'm a healthy, active seventy-five-year-old lady born without direction finders. I'm looking for a strong old man to go mountain hiking with me because I get lost alone, hate snakes, and can't keep my food out of the reach of bears.

All of us need to do more mountain hiking or an equivalent, get out in the wilds, sight a grizzly, and encounter a long, colorful snake. Our lives become too safe, too predictable, too tame. However, what we really want is to climb life's mountains and hills without direction finders at all.

Most of the time we know exactly where we're going in the morning, at noon, and at night. Our travel route is as predictable as a sunset. There's no question about whom we will see, or where, or why. There are no risks on the horizon. No strangers. Our lives become as cut-and-dried as if they had been sitting out on the kitchen sink. Let's throw away direction finders and go hiking in a real wilderness.

I'm ready to start fresh. I'll step into the wilderness and follow my instincts.

NOVEMBER 12

Three old people live in a house three houses up the street from mine. They are one man and two women. I understand the man is married to one of the women, and the other is her sister. They are quiet as church mice, secretive, never mix with neighbors, and this disturbs me.

Secretly, in some inner chamber of the heart, we seem to yearn for everybody to be the same. Is this a reason why diversity so often troubles and threatens us?

People are different. When our own differentness is called into question, we appreciate it when *our* individuality is respected. We have our own tastes, ideas, and feelings. We don't wish to be destroyed in an impersonal melting pot.

Neither do most other people. Some people want to be alone, others desire to be out in a crowd. Some cherish ethnic, religious, cultural tokens of diversity that become personal symbols of identity. There is plenty of room for both. Instead of being disturbed by obvious manifestations of diversity, we should be grateful for our own freedom, and support the freedom of others.

How has conformity kept me from my own path?
I'll respect difference where I find it, in myself, and in others.

Kunta burst suddenly into tears, as much in fear as in grief. Soon men came with a large, freshly split log and set it down in front of the hut. Kunta watched as the women brought out and laid on the log's flat surface the body of his grandmother, enclosed from her neck to her feet in a white cotton winding cloth.

ALEX HALEY

Many of us encounter death initially in the passing of a grandmother or grandfather.

Death seems awesome and unfriendly to us. What can we make of it when we're children, confronting death for the first time? That initial meeting stays in our mind for the rest of our life.

But then, we must meet death for the second time. The third. The tenth. Perhaps the hundredth in this age of AIDS. We become more familiar with it. Gradually it reveals itself as a natural part of life. Emily Dickinson revealed in a poem how we may one day end up having a far more intimate encounter with death. We may climb into a carriage and ride with death. Hopefully the ride will be a peaceful and gentle one.

I'll accustom myself to every stage of life. I won't be afraid of death.

NOVEMBER 14

I was imprisoned in that moment, bound hand and foot, an iron collar around my neck.

SIMONE DE BEAUVOIR

There are moments when we seem to be lost. Where is hope in any tangible form when everything horrible has happened to us? We seem to lack any semblance of control.

A picture comes to my mind. Suppose we have permitted ourselves to be painted into a corner of a room. The entire floor is freshly painted. We're standing alone in a distant corner, scared to death, and now the paint is slopping up against our shoes. What to do? Take a giant leap. Escape from the deadly corner. Jump across the room and through an open door. Claim freedom.

In moments of abject and cruel enslavement that seem to touch our lives we can break loose. Sometimes it's as simple as communicating the truth about what we feel. Letting people know. Breaking the bonds. Saying "This is it!" Moving on.

I have the power to change my life. My spirit claims freedom.

NOVEMBER 15

In the primitive world, where people live closer
to the earth and much nearer to the stars,
every inner and outer act combines to form
the single harmony, life. . . . They do not, as
many civilized people do, neglect the truth of
the physical for the sake of the mind.

LANGSTON HUGHES

Some people make the mistake of trying to live ninety-
nine percent in the mind, and one percent in the body.

There is *no* healthy balance in such an arrangement.
It's crazy. It denies the possibility of harmony. Accompa-
nying it generally is a wild drive for success that is de-
signed to eliminate every obstacle that stands in its way.

As a result, a person becomes machine-like. Such factors as feelings, relationship, love, children, and friendship become disposable items. They matter only if they
can be utilized as a means to an end, perhaps even an in-
come tax deduction. Denial of life becomes the norm.
But we need to affirm life. We need to live as close to the
earth as we can, commune with the stars whenever possible, and strive for harmony in our inner and outer life.

When am I living in the mind, and when in the body?
How do the scales tip in my life? Today, I'll focus on
my life as a physical animal.

I've got lots of time on my hands. One thing I do is build little monuments on my front lawn. I made a sculpture out of an old birdhouse, my old motorcycle goggles, and a bunch of model plane wings. People probably think I'm nuts.

One of the best things in life is to be creative. Another is to be ourself, unself-consciously and honestly.

It's sad when we don't express ourself, show our real feelings, or have the guts to do creative things because we fear others may laugh at us and fail to understand what we're doing.

If they don't get the point, it's their loss—not ours, unless we make the fatal error of worrying about what they'll say about us. Once we start doing that, there's no end to our dilemma. We can't ever please everybody else. We will never be fully accepted and understood by everybody. Some will understand us and *not* accept us. The beginning of wisdom is to accept ourself and give full rein to any forms of creativity that might grow out of us.

I'll nurture my creative impulse as I would a threatened species. I won't be curtailed by images or opinions.

NOVEMBER 17

Do you think we'll ever get back to the land of our dreams?

Nostalgia beckons in all of our lives. It's as if there were an archetypal dream we all share, filled with old-fashioned virtue and rugged adventure, and it tugs hard at the edges of our reality.

Yet the dream needs to be alive in the present, filled with the most compelling contemporary images as well as fragments from our past imagination. Our necessity is to live fully in the present. An understanding of the past is absolutely necessary, but romanticizing it can prove deadly.

We cannot get back to anything. As the author Thomas Wolfe pointed out, we can't go home again. Sometimes we want it so badly that we can see an old house as if it were here in the present, smell past kitchen warmth, look at smoke rise from a chimney. It's essential for us to honor the past, and love what is best about it, while using that experience to forge ahead in our present life.

What would it take to make this the land of my dreams? How could I come closer? Today, I'm thinking of how to get there, not how to go back.

Lately I've found myself thinking of a man I loved nearly thirty years ago. Somehow, despite all the intervening events, I realize I never loved anyone else so purely and totally as I loved him. I'd give anything to be able to find him again and tell him so.

An ideal, especially one in the past, can seem purer than the driven snow, untainted by the pressures and necessities of life.

It's all right for us to hold onto such an ideal, and give it a place in our life, as long as we connect it to reality. For example, we may remember fondly, even passionately, someone we loved many years ago. In our present recollection, he or she may seem nearly perfect.

But no one is. Over the passing years we've changed, radically and in endless small ways. So has the person we remember, who may no longer be alive; or, if living, may be in a happy, stable relationship. More to the point, it is not fair to compare our past ideal with a flesh-and-blood person presently in our life. It's far more important to love the person who is *here*.

I won't judge the present by the past. The past may seem perfect; the present is here. Today, I welcome it with open arms.

I've tried my damnedest not to get old. This in itself is a tough job. I don't mean age old, because that's an honorable thing. I mean attitude old.

ROBERT R. MCCAMMON

Dictionary definitions of *old* send mixed signals.

They refer, on the one hand, to *feeble, dilapidated,* and *worn out.* But then, on the other hand, they refer to *mature, practical, sensible,* and *a ripe old age.* Obviously, no simple umbrella defines *old.* We need to be considerably more specific.

Whether we use old to indicate age or attitude, we must make clear exactly what we mean. I know an eighty-five-year-old man who is mentally and spiritually younger than springtime. I know a seventy-five-year-old woman who appears to be physically and mentally near her prime. To cite their age as a kind of proof text doesn't tell their true story. It's entirely possible to be as old as the hills, as the saying goes, and at the same time be as young as a new moon.

Today, I'll be myself, and leave it to others to classify.

Twenty-six years ago I was virtually at the end of my rope, lost in a sea of alcoholism. Now I am in recovery.

At particular moments life can seem hopeless. Apparently (we feel) there is no light at the end of the tunnel. We seem to have lost everything. We're hurt and embarrassed, and it seems we've given up.

It is precisely at such moments that the great turning points in our life may occur. We discern a semblance of light at the faraway end of an unimaginably dark tunnel. We catch a glimmer of hope, are touched by a spark of understanding.

Aliveness intervenes, and we're a bit like Lazarus walking outside his tomb. Everything has not been solved. Much work remains to be done. Transformation will absorb countless hours, days, and years of our life, a step at a time. Yet peace exists where it did not. The sun has come out. It feels good to be alive.

Today, I congratulate myself for the changes I've made. I recognize the job continues.

NOVEMBER 21

Father Fitzgibbon might have been any brogue-rippling old male biddy. But as [Barry] Fitzgerald portrays him—senile, vain, childish, stubborn, good, bewildered, stupid— he is the quintessence of the pathos, dignity and ludicrousness which old age can display.

JAMES AGEE (ON *GOING MY WAY*)

Old age is a mixed bag. So is middle age. So is youth.

Any of these can be looked at critically, humorously, judgmentally, sensitively; with a predetermined agenda, in terms of pathology or ordinary human behavior. If one is limited to cliches, old age can be seen as a bewildering tragedy, middle age as "mid-life crisis," and youth as wanton irresponsibility.

In each of the stages of human life there may be found pathos, and dignity, ludicrousness, and more. It seems preferable to try to see an individual instead of a representative of an age group. Otherwise, we're prone to end up with either the *best* or the *worst* example of a type, and miss an individual.

To hell with stupid and judgmental cliches. I'll strive to be who I am, the best I'm able.

NOVEMBER 22

My aunt is a lively eighty-eight-year-old woman who is a strong survivor, including being stubborn as hell. I look in on her every day, cook for her occasionally, and talk to her on the phone regularly. I'm her only relative. But I wonder if my aunt should continue to live in her home or move to a retirement home. I am the one who apparently must make that decision.

Taking life a day at a time, and doing the best we can, is a sterling idea.

Sometimes we can't plan ahead effectively. Nor do we need to. We don't know what the future holds. We continue to live in the present, under the best conditions we can muster.

The biggest decision can be the choice to take life a day at a time. This means pouring our available energy into it. We cease second-guessing and looking over our shoulder to see if something is gaining on us. We quit wondering about *this* alternative or *that* one, shuffling them like cards in a deck, and concentrate on feeling gratitude for what we have in the present moment.

I can't control tomorrow. I offer thanks for this period of grace in which I can move and have my being.

For the Queen quite simply looks her best
with a diamond crown on her head, loaded
with royal jewels, and seated on a throne. No
longer young and never a beauty, she puts
beautiful young women around her in the
shade. She has the classic handsome back, the
impressive stately bosom for roped pearls, the
tractable curled coiffure of another
generation, and the fine old-fashioned skin
that companioned them.

JANET FLANNER

Beauty is ageless, has little or nothing to do with pretti-
ness, and is at its best when in a natural setting that is
true to itself.

We admire beauty, but seldom realize that in an older
person it becomes a matter of poise, bearing, innate
style, essential dignity, and finally, complete inner naturalness.

Beauty is cultivated, as is a rose. It is to be celebrated.
Beauty is one of the wonders of the world, yet simplicity
always underlies whatever artifice it wears.

Inner naturalness and innate simplicity: today, I want
to find and cultivate these within myself.

My sixty-first birthday. I am now definitely beyond middle age and well on my way to the sere and yellow, and I find it very difficult to believe. I feel very little different from twenty years ago, or even thirty!

NOËL COWARD

Discerning that we've departed middle age for older status is one of life's turning points.

We notice it gradually. The way people look at us. Buying a ticket for a senior (us) at the movies. Asking the doctor an altogether different set of questions during the checkup. Being fitted for new glasses.

The rub is that, at first, we don't feel older. We may even resent the implication that we are. "Are you calling me a senior?" Then, with the passing of time, we come to realize that we do feel older, after all. When we learn to accept this, it's better for us and everybody else.

I acknowledge growing older—and I marvel at my ability to do so.

Dying, would he have wondered, could he have, whether his work would live?

MARK SCHORER

Virtually everybody wonders what part of his or her life will continue, and matter, after death.

Emperors built gigantic monuments to survive them. Creative geniuses leave a legacy of music, art, or literature. Many people expect to be remembered always by their family, to be at least a branch of a family tree.

What we do in the arena of work is frequently the treasure where our heart is to be found. We pour time and energy, muscle and soul, into ambitious, self-constructed monuments. We like to think our work will be remembered as a symbol of our discipline, commitment, zeal, competitiveness, skills, and passion. Usually it is not. Yet, although we cannot build a pyramid, we yearn for a form of immortality on the earth. I wonder why so many forget the greatest memorial is to live on in the heart of another human being who loves us, remembers us fondly, and is deeply grateful for our life.

Today, I'll think about the monuments I've built
I'll make sure they're founded in the heart

NOVEMBER 26

I'm seventy-one and recently fell and hurt my back. My doctor doesn't want me to drive a car anymore. But my car was my connection to life outside my home. I hate the idea of losing my independence and having to rely on other people for help.

It's an illusion whenever we believe we are free and not dependent on other people.

Our life is tightly networked with the lives of others. We breathe the same air, drink the same water, eat the same food, walk on the same earth, use the same energy, watch the same TV, read the same press, vote in the same election, cheer in the same stadium, get ready for the same departure with death, and share the same enterprise called life.

And all of us rely on others for every possible kind of help. It seems apparent that frontier days, accompanied by their fierce stance of independence, are long-gone relics from the past. It is a sign of maturity to welcome help from others as well as to offer it willingly.

I may have to rely on others. I won't let that become a frightening prospect.

Isak Dinesen was in no way intimidated
by her death. She went to smell the linden
blossoms and to hear the nightingales,
knowing it was for the last time, but this sense
of finality was not morbid: it heightened the
moment for her, and for those who shared it.

JUDITH THURMAN

Some of us are given the opportunity to know death is coming, so this lets us prepare for it. Others meet death abruptly, without warning.

When there is ample time to prepare for death's coming, we can revisit old memories, read past correspondence, write to friends, see others, collect our thoughts, meditate and say our prayers, pay old emotional debts, extend forgiveness and receive it, and engage in a careful leave-taking.

Yet death can move into our life at *any* time. It's a good idea to be ready for it always. Make our peace. Do the necessary homework. Try to be on good terms with the leading players in our life's drama. Look backward, look forward, and be prepared to depart in the present moment.

I can't expect the luxury of a movie-scripted death. I won't put off my preparations, both inner and practical.

NOVEMBER 28

Our three children are grown and married, but they still rely on my husband and me to be their parents as if they were helpless kids. We're sick of the whole thing and want to live our old age out happily. Why don't they grow up? Why don't they treat us with gratitude for all we've done for them?

All of us are conditioned by numerous forces to see primary people in our life in terms of patriarchal and matriarchal roles.

A mother is *a mother*, not simply a close friend or loved one. A father is *a father*. These roles carry a lot of hereditary and emotional luggage.

A mother, then, is supposed to act like *a mother;* this can severely limit her freedom to be herself. A father is similarly fenced in, facing the same kind of limitations. It can take years for a child to reach a place of enough maturity and freedom to be able in turn to grant freedom to parents to be *themselves*.

Today, I give myself and others a clean slate. I'll try responding without old expectations. I'll provide novelty.

The characteristic plaint of the older woman—
"I would rather die than be a burden to my
children"—bespeaks a terror at an impending
loss of control over one's life in the face of a
world turned upside down, a world in which
someone whose own life has been devoted to
caring for others now needs caring for.

SUSAN WEIDMAN SCHNEIDER

Virtually everyone must face the possibility that he or
she will need caring for at some future stage in life.

Our introduction to the problem occurs when one of
our own parents or grandparents requires care. Trying to
make sense out of possible alternatives, often we feel
we're caught between a rock and a hard place. What to
do? What's fair? What's right?

Always, as we make a decision about a loved one's
care, we're aware that what we're doing may presage our
own presence in a similar situation later. It is a moment
of stark revelation. There's a story of a son who carries a
blanket to his aged father on a freezing night. The father
cuts the blanket into two pieces, and gives his son one.
"This is for you when you are old and cold, and in need
of a blanket."

I'll give what care I can, gladly, knowing I may need it
myself one day.

NOVEMBER 30

As you grow old, years may get shorter and shorter: but moments can be just as long as ever.

JAMES GOULD COZZENS

Time plays fascinating games with us.

When we are young, time unfolds before us like a winding road, going on forever. Our view is changed when we start work and face the daily demands of a job. Time becomes something to wrestle with. Another unforgettable lesson about time is the birth of a baby after nine short months.

Growing older, the years seem to race by. Where did they go? Yet moments are different. They can seem to creep along like centuries when we're waiting for a lunch break, move at a snail's pace when we drive in heavy traffic. In the dark of the night moments can become ghostlike when we awake and start thinking about myriad things. Talk about existentialism. Will dawn ever come? I guess the answer is that we should stretch our years as far as we can, expanding every possible moment. We should diligently compress our moments, moving them expeditiously at a quick, lively pace.

Today, I'll stop and appreciate the present moment I'll make it last.

When one reaches one's sixties it is difficult at first not to feel a grievous sense of shock at the disintegration of the Clan, the ever-increasing frequency of the departure of one's friends, hopefully to Paradise.

LAURENCE OLIVIER

I remember when my ninety-five-year-old mother lost five of her close friends within the span of a single year.

The more we hear about friends who have died, the closer we move toward the day when we have an appointment with death ourself. Reading obituaries, we notice the age of the deceased and the cause of death. Today the majority of persons who die under forty have succumbed to AIDS.

Old friends are an integral part of our life, but it's important for all of us to reach out and make new friends. It is not harder to do this as we grow older, despite reports to the contrary. Countless people are lonely and in need of friendship. They have many gifts to offer. It is selfish of us when we turn our back on the possibility of a new friendship. We need it just as much as anyone else does.

I won't let the loss of old friends isolate me from the joys of new ones.

DECEMBER 2

My husband is having an affair at seventy-two. He was indiscreet enough to take her out to dinner at a restaurant where a friend of mine ran into them. My friend called me first thing the next morning to tell me about it. My husband is a doddering old fool and I could wring his neck.

There are reasons why people do things. It's important for us to know the reasons as well as the things.

Sometimes we share in the responsibility, even though we don't want to admit it. We may not even grasp it. Yet this doesn't save us from participating in the consequences.

If someone else does something that hurts us, part of our responsibility is to bring it out into the open with that person. Not sweep it under a rug. Not pretend it isn't there. Not wish it would go away. And a sense of humor may be the most essential ingredient in a situation laced with misunderstanding and bitterness. After all, the human comedy has the longest run of all.

Today, I'll face the truth. I'll try to see the humor as well as the sadness of it.

DECEMBER 3

The judge was an old man; so old, he seemed to have outlived time and change and death. His parrot-face and parrot-voice were dry, like his old, heavily-veined hands. His scarlet robe clashed harshly with the crimson of the roses. He had sat for three days in the stuffy court, but he showed no sign of fatigue.

DOROTHY L. SAYERS

Appearances have a way of hiding the truth. This is why we should not rely on them, but take a closer look.

We all know that glamour can be skin deep. What appear to be jewels may be paste. What is called antipasto may bear little resemblance to it. Social behavior hailed as chic may lack the rudiments of good manners.

A person who appears on the surface to be very old—even ancient—may possess deep reserves of strength so great as to shatter the devil's armor or vanquish a mere gladiator. Despite its appearance of virility and vigor, youth does not possess maturity and experience. It lacks primal strength, finely honed awareness, and focused energy. These spring only from the soul.

I won't be fooled or put off by surfaces. I'll poke around beneath appearances to see the truth.

My voyage is at its end. I think how glorious to grow old!

FREDERIC PROKOSCH

Aging conjures up different pictures. One is of an old, majestic tree that has weathered many seasons of sun, ice, snow, and rain. Another is of an elderly person whom we feel privileged to know, someone who combines rare humor with fine candor, a rich taste for life with a remarkable hint of youthful vigor.

It is a blessing to have lived such a full and rewarding life, filled with friends, ideas, passions, and challenges. Life seems to possess its own seasons, ranging from birth and youth to maturity and old age. At its best it has known the rigors of winter and promises of springtime, the peace of summer and sharp expectation of autumn.

With the approach of the final season there is a sense of coming closure. When confronted by the end of life, fortunate people can sense its approach and offer thanks for their experiences. They can marvel at the wonder that they got here, and rejoice in it.

If my life is a voyage, where am I now? Where do I still want to go? Today, I chart my voyage anew.

DECEMBER 5

The night Aurora had her stroke she dreamed that a mad dog bit her. It was a small, savage black dog, and it came at her snapping while she was on her knees in the backyard, mending a flower bed.

LARRY MCMURTRY

When bad things happen, whether in our lives or in our dreams, we call them nightmares.

They seem to be things that we associate with the night instead of the day. Shadows hover about such things; we cannot see them clearly. They are frightening, threatening, and strike terror at our heart. We have no control over them at all.

But then the deep shadows of the night give way to a new dawn. A sense of perspective returns. We can see the extent of our damage, assess it, and our life goes on. Reason replaces terror. If a nightmare occurs in a dream, we focus on it one last time and let it go. If a nightmare occurs in our life, we begin to live with it as a part of ourself that requires healing.

I'll look for the interesting angle in a bad dream. What am I trying to tell myself?

I am HIV-positive and have the AIDS virus. I have been with my lover for eight years and we plan a church blessing of our union. My lover's dad and mom have accepted our invitation to come to the service. My sister will attend, but my father refuses to come. This means my mom won't be there either. It makes me sad to see my family split like this.

We have to make decisions in our life that are not dependent on the feelings and wishes of others, no matter how close they may be.

When we decide what we're going to do, we've really announced that we are self-reliant, know our own mind, have set our course, and are not waiting for a U.N. resolution to provide us with a mandate.

After we make our decision, it's up to others to react as they wish. We should be ready for a variety of responses, ranging from negative to positive ones. It's important to respect the feelings of others and try to understand them. A helpful way to do this is to try looking at our situation through their eyes. However, this does not in any way affect our decision. It's been made.

I'll expect the best response from others. I'll be grateful when I'm right. But I'll do what I know is right regardless.

I helped the old lady do her work, helped her wash her heavy quilts that had gone two years without washing, to her despair, because she had no help with them, and can no longer lift them alone from the water and get them on the line. She cried when I left!

MARJORIE KINNAN RAWLINGS

Helping others is one of the greatest things we can ever do while we're in the world. It requires a certain disciplined selflessness, placing the needs of others equal to our own or ahead of them. It means going the extra mile; it's beautiful to behold. This kind of selflessness can occur when we're able to let our concern for others replace our ever insistent self-interest. We open up our heart in the act of giving.

We know from experience that when we stay bone selfish and refuse to give, we don't receive. It's that simple and is one of life's basic lessons. On the other hand, when we give we find that the gift we put out there for others can come back to us tenfold. We also receive satisfaction, fulfillment, and a sense of worth.

Today, I'll look for the satisfaction in giving.

DECEMBER 8

I have worked hard all my life. I thought old age would mean I was finally free to enjoy my life. But I find my children's lives are coming apart. My son just got divorced after twenty-six years of marriage. My daughter's life is in a shambles—bad husband, unemployment, sick kids. I wish I could live my life instead of theirs.

It's said we come into the world alone and depart it the same way.

There is, in any case, an awareness of our own identity. We are not simply a daughter, a son, a mother, a father, a wife, a husband, a sister, a brother, a boss, an employee, a neighbor, a youth, an elder. We are highly individual persons as well as incredibly unique women and men.

A corollary is that we have our life to live. We can't live anyone else's. No one else can live ours. It can be a splendid thing to sacrifice for others and give, give, give. Yet we need to receive as well as to give. If we don't respect our life, how can we respect anyone else's? We have to live our own life instead of the lives of others.

Today, I'll focus on living my own life. I won't attempt to live the lives of others.

> The canard that my vocal chords are giving me trouble is pure invention.
>
> ENRICO CARUSO

Learning how to deal with gossip and the spread of untrue, even damaging rumors is necessary for us. If we possess thin skins, how do we fend off attacks?

Getting into a big fight over gossip and rumors only serves to give them more attention and publicity. The more uproar we create in reacting to them, the more we arouse emotions, then suspicions. The best way to refute a lie is to live the truth. In other words, to be a walking contradiction of untrue stories told about us. For example, if we're accused of cheating, the best defense is to be known as indisputably honest. This makes an accuser appear ridiculous.

The other side of the coin is that we should never initiate unfair gossip and untrue rumors about anyone else. If we hear them, it's our responsibility to nip them in the bud. The buck stops here.

I'm going to remember the harm words can do, and stick to the truth.

DECEMBER 10

My wife and I were married for thirty-two years when she said she didn't love me anymore. She rejected me and wanted to live alone. I was stunned. I lost my self-respect. I moved out, left her the house, rented a small walk-up apartment, divided our savings with her. We have no children. Now I am without companionship or love and have nothing to live for.

Life can sometimes resemble the *Titanic*. When the proud, seemingly secure ocean liner hit an iceberg in the mid-Atlantic, it sank. There are moments when we seem to be sinking, too.

We can be surprised by what life brings us! Despair and a sense of terrible loss are often first reactions. But we don't have the luxury of time for these if our ship is sinking in icy water amid raging waves. We've got to find a lifeboat and make our way to safety and survival.

The instinct to go on living is our best ally in terms of adversity. It pumps adrenalin, keeps our mind alert, and makes us realize we face a truly awesome challenge. We have no time to indulge feelings of self-pity. We've got to fight against adversity and get our life back.

I'm ready for any challenge. I have survived adversity before, and I can do it again.

DECEMBER 11

For many old people, eating is the only pleasure left, as were the "endless dishes" and "unceasing cups of wine" to the aged Ulysses.

M. F. K. FISHER

Young people, on the whole, seem to eat larger quantities of food than older ones do. Many of us recall the sensuous eating scene in the film *Tom Jones,* where a robust dinner increasingly took on the shape of a lively orgy.

Generally the appetite for eating of an older woman or man becomes somewhat diminished in quantity, while perhaps more sophisticated and discerning when it comes to quality. There has simply been wider experience with great menus, recipes, sauces, and wines over a lifetime.

Enjoyment is measured by appreciation; appreciation is measured by experience. Ideally, older people can enjoy—and appreciate—a work of art in the form of a garden, a book, a concert, a tree, the stars, rain, sunshine, and a lovely, memorable meal.

Have I forgotten the pleasure of a simple meal? Today, I'll break bread with a friend. I'll savor this ritual.

My husband is a workaholic. He's sixty-eight and seems to think he's twenty-eight, judging by the hours he works and the stress he's under. He keeps talking about the likelihood he'll die first and I will be a widow. I wish I could pick him up by the nape of his neck and get him out of his damned office.

We can't teach an old dog new tricks. Nor can we provide a new scenario for another person's existence.

So, when confronted by a characteristic or a trait in another person that's driving us crazy, we have at least two choices. We can make it the center of our life, allowing it to become an obsessive cause of anxiety. Or, we can realize it is out of our capacity to change it. Then we place it on the periphery of our life, readjust our priorities, and no longer let it drive us nuts.

When we can't change someone else or difficult circumstances, we can change ourself and the way we look at a problem. We should never let it dominate our thinking, our feelings, our perspective—our life.

I cannot change another. Only myself. Today, I'll work to change my own perspective on an old problem.

DECEMBER 13

He wished that he could talk to his father about his great-grandfather, about his father's early life. But it never seemed possible and he knew that what held him back was less an inhibiting shyness than the fear that, even if he broke through this strange barrier of reticence and inarticulateness, there would be nothing there.

P. D. JAMES

It is astonishing how often we do not speak the truth in love. We allow a moment of possible communication to pass by forever.

Two people in a relationship wear masks, say lines that seem to have been scripted by a playwright, wear masks, and all the while adamantly refuse to tell the truth. A father and a son, each yearning for intimacy with the other, make small talk and remain strangers. A mother and a daughter, locked into roles as if by a jailer, stay at an emotional distance.

There seems to be an awful fear that, having risked communicating, there will be only nothingness, emptiness, a void. Therefore, fearing it, we both create and perpetuate it. Reaching out from vulnerability is difficult. It is far more difficult, however, to live with the awareness that a door has been closed and locked, and may never be opened again.

Today, I'll risk vulnerability. I'll ask the question I've been holding back.

DECEMBER 14

All of us always thought my father was a neat guy. He died last year. Now mom has told us he was bisexual and slept with a number of men as well as women. She said he also misused alcohol and sometimes beat her. She is fit to be tied because she repressed her feelings so long.

One of the biggest mysteries of them all—right up there with Sherlock Holmes and *Murder, She Wrote*—is why people repress feelings over a long period of time.

It requires so much energy to repress feelings! And, worst of all, the feelings that got repressed have to surface somewhere else, with Lord knows what ramifications and repercussions.

Think of the damage done, the sadness caused because reality was not confronted openly and mutually, with the hope that something practical could be done about the whole thing. Why don't we learn, and not repeat old tragedies?

I won't shroud any part of my life in darkness. I'll leave behind no hurtful surprises.

DECEMBER 15

Never even had no friends. Nobody. Just laid up there in that room sucking up the sneaky pete. Used to drink a gallon a day. I think he lived off his social security.

JOSEPH WAMBAUGH

A wasted life is one of the saddest things. It breaks our heart when we see it at close range.

We find caring isn't enough. We learn that we can't help anyone turn a life around unless the person wishes to do so. There has to be a strong internal motivation to change old habits, cease a pattern of self-destruction, and somehow start a new way of living.

Yes, we can be supportive. We can provide material and spiritual help. We can walk the extra mile. But we can't work magic. We can't bring the genie out of the bottle to perform miracles on demand. The person who has been self-destructive—and still is—must own up to it, decide to seek help, ask for the intervention of a greater power than his or hers, and start moving toward recovery a step at a time.

From whom have I flinched? Could I make a difference, for us both? Where I can help, I'll offer support.

DECEMBER 16

I worship my dad. However, he's an absolute stranger to me. I'm in my thirties, ambitious, work too hard, but am determined to get to the top. My dad had a chance for success when he was young, blew it, and ended up a guy who's hurting and bruised. He's a has-been. I want to make it big for both of us.

We can't go all the way back in our history, or anyone else's, and rewrite it.

Nor can we assume we understand anyone else's past or how best to deal with it. A principal reason is that many herstories and histories include emotional traumas, painful breakups and divorces, difficult professional experiences, and unresolved dilemmas that we can't see.

It's particularly dangerous if we think we understand someone else's pain when we actually don't. The next fatal step is to prescribe a solution for the person on the basis of our flawed analysis. We may offer encouragement, support, friendship, solace, time, energy, and love—but the buck has to stop here when we feel like playing god.

Today, I'll take a hard look at what drives me. I'll accept the limits of what I can do.

In the years since I began following the ways of my grandmothers I have come to value the teachings, stories, and daily examples of living which they shared with me.

BEVERLY HUNGRY WOLF

The world was not born yesterday. There is an accumulated wisdom that is a treasure.

Whenever we lose sight of history, we face the prospect of repeating it. It would be foolhardy for any generation to decide to dispense with the past and start over from scratch.

Folk wisdom is one of the great sources of learning about everything from spirituality to caring for the body, eating the right food to creating art. We have an incredible heritage that provides us with information, wisdom, and inspiration. In stories out of the past we can find ourself, our dilemmas and possible alternatives, and fresh paths to follow in our life. In examples of people who went before us we can discover sources of strength that help us to make difficult decisions, become better persons, and grow to maturity.

Where is the tradition in my family? Is there any knowledge to be tapped? Today, I'll look for that wisdom.

My mother hates my wife. She is making it almost impossible for me to be a good son because she keeps insulting my wife and trying to drive a wedge between us. The tension is unbearable.

Some human situations seem more insoluble than others. We find that we're trapped between a rock and a hard place. Nothing gives at all. We search in vain for any answer, let alone an easy one.

While there may not be a single answer, there can be alternative ways to approach our problem. We need to examine these and make choices. For example, given a crisis between two people in our life, we can come to each of them alone and attempt to have a rational discussion about what's wrong, and why. After that, perhaps we need to bring together the two people who are engaged in a crisis. We can ascertain if either one wishes to be isolated with bitterness. If not, it's necessary to find a way to make peace, even a fragile and temporary one.

Today, I'll end an old tension. I won't choose between two unacceptables. I'll make a new way.

I see a society where the structural revolution has provided more choices and more varied roles for older people. A society where lifelong learning replaces the lockstep of traditional education, a society where the burdens of the middle generation are spread over the life course.

MATILDA RILEY

This is an exceptionally exciting and productive time to be an older woman or man.

It's hard for us to imagine the way human life apparently used to be structured. A person's place in the world was set in cement within the limitations of a rigid class society. Women's and men's roles were inflexible. Opportunity was limited to the privileged. Beliefs were not supposed to be questioned. The elderly were frequently ostracized, denied their rights, and treated cruelly.

Now there is growing awareness of the dynamics of growing older. There is more care and concern. Health care is more available. Opportunities abound for older women and men in continuing education, volunteerism, recreation, and work. A richer life is possible.

Am I taking advantage of the good things this time has to offer? Today, I'm going to set about enriching my life

For thirty years my husband and I lived for each other alone. "Let's shut out the world," he'd always say, drawing the blinds. Now, without him, I'm finding it's not so easy to let the world back in.

It takes a fine balancing act to draw satisfaction and enjoyment from our personal life and, at the same time, to honor and serve the world around us.

Ultimately, they don't represent an either/or choice at all. Unless we live in the world actively, we deny ourself the full meaning of a rich life. If we don't put aside time and energy for a full personal life, we can easily become embittered and end up not having a whole life at all.

The secret seems to be sharing our personal life, not hoarding it for ourself. When two people attempt to exist in isolation, they commit a fatal error. Personal life needs to be opened up to include the world. This doesn't mean all of it rushing in in one fell swoop, but entering gradually, wisely, richly.

Today, I step down off the funeral pyre.

Jenny Garp would outlive them all. If she had been at the party where her brother choked to death, she probably could have saved him. At least she would have known exactly what to do.

JOHN IRVING

In most of our lives there is someone absolutely marvelous who treats age with the utmost grace and appears to be literally indestructible.

Usually this is an older woman or man who possesses a deep reservoir of humor, mysterious sources of energy, a bold zest for life, and a disciplined ability to greet each dawn with work to do. Someone like this can even make an unsuspecting teenager resemble the ancient mariner.

Curiously, such a person, who obviously lives life to the fullest, also seems the best prepared for eternity. There is no apparent fear of death. In fact, his or her insatiable joy in living translates into an exuberant expectation about the life that is to follow.

I'll look for the wisdom and experience around me. I'll honor it.

DECEMBER 22

My lover and I broke up four years ago and I've been living alone. I'm a sixty-seven-year-old lesbian and a successful businesswoman who has a workaholic streak. Recently I met another woman who loves me and has asked to make a life with me. But I'm afraid. I don't know if I dare risk a new relationship.

One of the worst mistakes we can ever make is to give up on life.

The energy and momentum of life is one of its greatest surprises. To cooperate with it is important. This is an acknowledgment of its power and potential for us. There are times when life itself seems to have a plan for us, surpassing anything we can dream up. Our positive response is needed.

If we hang back, mistrust possibility, deny the lovely meaning of serendipity in our life, and announce our best days and years are behind us, we put up roadblocks. We don't need them! They get in the way of everything. Better to let the way ahead lie open and unhindered. Then we can dare, and take a risk. We can even believe it's not a risk at all.

I won't hang back from opportunity because of age. I'm alive, and I deserve to go on *living*.

The world is incomprehensible. We won't ever understand it; we won't ever unravel its secrets. Thus we must treat it as it is, a sheer mystery.

CARLOS CASTANEDA

What is sheer delight about the world is its refusal to give up its secrets.

Some people climb Mt. Everest or plumb the depths of the ocean, travel in outer space or search archaeological ruins. All this merely touches the surface of serious exploration of life.

We are confronted with sheer mystery when we experience love, discover our own naked vulnerability in the arms of another person who is yet another mystery; when we awaken slowly to the incomprehensible sound in the stillness that accompanies freshly fallen snow; when we witness birth or death; when we look at the intricate detail of a gnarled tree and perceive the secret of creation, perseverance, and the whole universe; when hope enters a room like a breath of air and dissipates despair; when loving replaces self-hatred, rage, and violence.

Today, I acknowledge my sheer ignorance in the face of so much mystery. And praise it.

My mother's drinking problem got worse and worse. She was an alcoholic when my husband died unexpectedly three years ago. I desperately needed her wisdom and help. Almost as if by a miracle, my mother stopped drinking, and her support made all the difference in my life.

We tend to forget how closely interwoven our life is with the lives of others, especially loved ones and close friends.

A tremendous challenge arises for us when someone close is in terrible trouble or faces a life crisis. It can bring out the best in us when we attempt to offer help and everything we can, at the cost of our own convenience and resources.

At such a moment we may rise to levels of maturity beyond our comprehension. While helping someone else, we've been helped immeasurably by our acts of generosity that were not rooted in self-interest. A call for help can cut through tangled emotions and bring out the best in our human spirit.

Miracles have to start somewhere. Today, I'll answer a call for help.

Up to his last days Cavafy was writing, and it is said that while on his deathbed he asked Rika Singopoulos to look up a reference in the municipal library that he wanted for his last poem.

ROBERT LIDDELL

It is vitally important that older people remain active, pursuing a primary interest or occupation, continuing to be creative and responsive to life.

This involves having a compelling reason to get up in the morning, something to do, someone to see. Life should continue to be not just interesting, but downright fascinating.

We need to know that what we do matters—in some context, or to somebody, or to us. The odds are we're not going to paint the Sistine Chapel, compose a sequel to *Aïda,* open up a five-star restaurant, or write a book that sits atop the bestseller list for sixteen months. So what? We're significant. No one else is quite like us. What we do reflects us.

What *matters?* Today, I'll look into my deepest heart. And I'll act on what I find there.

I'm sixty-five, a woman who is alone, and I work in the realty business. I work my butt off, and love every minute of it. People keep asking me when I'm going to retire. Why should I? I think they'll have to carry me off.

One person's cup of tea is another person's gin martini or chocolate milkshake.

We like different things. Our tastes vary widely. So do our ambitions and goals. For example, one person genuinely wishes to retire at the earliest opportunity in order to develop new interests or even do nothing at all. Another person can't bear the idea of retiring, loves his or her work, and just keeps rolling along.

We should never try to force our view upon someone else's life. If a person wants to work until he or she drops, we can be supportive. If a person wishes to bail out and cease work as quickly as possible, we can be helpful. Rule one: If someone wants a cup of Earl Grey tea, don't serve a cup of espresso.

There's no one to measure myself against, no expectation to meet but my own. I'm moving straight ahead, on my own path.

DECEMBER 27

It reminds us of the one really hateful thing about life: that we must all depart from it eventually, or to state the matter more exactly, that it must depart from us, is departing from us.

GLENWAY WESCOTT

The one unmistakable, irrefutable thing about this life is that it's not permanent. It is transitory. We are in transition.

We came into this life in a dramatic moment called birth. We've had to learn everything from toilet skills to verbal skills to getting along with people. During our life tenure we've dealt with passion, lacerating hurt, quiet joy, betrayal, and forgiveness. Our education as earthlings has been more sophisticated and demanding than anything on Harvard's curriculum.

No one holds any presumption that he or she has permanent digs here. We're passing through. Yet most of us live this life as if it were going to last forever. Then, one day, it's over. To keep this from being hateful, we should live life to the hilt in its rapid passing, and spend some valuable time preparing to depart.

Here I am, alive and in the world, right now. It's all anyone has, and it's everything. I'm grateful.

A warm feeling swept over me. I felt good. I
thought, I didn't get rich and I didn't get
famous. Who cares? I had a good time trying.
I did as I liked.

LOUISE RANDALL PIERSON

Life is meant to be lived. We should really let it happen,
joyful about its mystery and awe, and quit looking over
our shoulder all the time. Who wants to turn into a pil-
lar of salt?

The big question is always: What do we want out of
life? Some people want power, position, big-time stuff,
and wads of dough. Ads and the media sell such imagery
all the time. That kind of glamour is on TV and the billboards. But we know, most of us, that such stuff often
leads to dead ends in life and a sharp denial of happiness.

Better to live life our way, whatever that means to
each of us, liking life, finding genuine fulfillment in it.
This has nothing to do with what other people think of
us. It has a lot to do with how we think of ourselves. If
we fail to become a person whom we like and respect,
what's the use?

Today, a pat on the back. I'm proud of the person
I've become.

DECEMBER 29

I could never forgive my father for walking away from our family when I was a kid. He deserted us, my mom, sister, and brother. I grew up, went to school, then went to work and got married. I always hated him for what he had done. Recently I went to visit him. He was very sick and about to die. We bonded at last. It gave me peace.

Life is full of fierce passions, big hurts, great joys, and lots of things beyond any easy understanding.

It's inevitable that we respond to life as passionately as life treats us. We say we'll "never forgive." We say we'll "fight to the finish." We say we're "bruised, bloodied, but unbowed." We say we'll "kill for what's right."

Our fiercest passions, however, seem gradually to give way to a glimmer of empathy and a streak of tenderness. We remember the good, not only the bad. We even learn to laugh in recollection of a difficult past event, instead of crying about it. Our focus shifts. It is an indication of maturity. It permits us to partake of the riches.

Today, I'm going to scrutinize an old wound and find forgiveness.

I want you to give up what you think you know and open to what you do not yet know. I want you to recognize and live in your spirit. I want you to burn up your past and live for what life may yet bring you—for the revelations it will bring you, if you dare to live for them.

ANDREW HARVEY

The best part of our life may be just around the next corner.

It's crucial that we retain our belief in this. Life thrusts us forward. The best part need not be buried in memories. Our validation should not be sought in former successes, joys, achievements, and friendships. In its mysterious and fascinating ways, life summons us to move ahead and discover ever new treasures of the spirit.

How can we live fully in hope, in love, and with faith? By taking risks. By continuing to grow as a person, never resting on past laurels. In order to claim our wholeness we must dare. We need to define what we have lacked up to now, what we want that we don't have, and what it will take to make us whole. This means being truly alive. This means being open to what we do not yet know.

I'll embrace life fully every day, with all the wisdom of my years, and all the innocence of a child. I'll begin *now*.

INDEX

fun Feb. 5, 14; Mar. 13; May 29

good-byes June 24
gossip Apr. 27; Dec. 10
grace Aug. 26
gratitude Mar. 3; Apr. 5; June 10; Aug. 4
grieving Feb. 2, 16; Aug. 7

happiness Jan. 24; Apr. 18
hell on earth Feb. 19
helping others Jan. 15, 21, Mar. 12, 21; Apr. 21; June 3; Dec. 8, 16, 25
honesty Feb. 12; Aug. 18, 24; Sept. 29; Dec. 3
hope Jan. 20; Feb. 10; Mar. 20; Apr. 25; May 15; June 15, 28; July 7, 29; Sept. 8; Oct. 18
humility Apr. 13

identity July 9
illness Aug. 27; Sept. 6, 15
image Jan. 5, 18; Feb. 13; May 2; June 7; July 14; Sept. 11; Oct. 15, 25; Nov 7; Dec. 4
imagination Oct. 2
immortality Nov. 26
impersonality Mar. 18
independence Oct. 12
indifference Mar. 9
inertia May 24
initiative Feb. 24

integrity Feb. 13; June 21, Aug. 10
involvement Aug 20

learning Jan. 25; Apr. 12
letting go Dec. 13, 17
life-expectancy Oct. 9
listening Feb. 8
living today Jan. 7, 9, 16; Feb 9, 18, 22; Mar. 2, 30; Apr. 14, 23; May 5; May 14; June 14, 30; July 12; Aug. 2; Sept. 18; Nov. 19, 23; Dec. 23, 31
loneliness Feb. 1, 26; Mar. 6; June 11; Aug. 3, 29; Sept. 5; Dec. 21
loss Sept. 20, 30; Oct. 5; Nov 5, 11
love Apr. 10; May 22; June 26; Sept. 3, 13; Oct. 7
loving life Feb. 27

mail July 16
maturity Jan. 3; Feb. 17; June 27; July 23
meaning Apr. 1; June 9, 20; July 5; Dec. 26
memory Mar. 17; May 18; June 13; Oct. 6, 17; Nov 10
miracles May 21
money Apr. 22; Oct. 3

nature Mar. 27; May 30; June 12; Dec. 24